AF471226

This & That

A Bead Pattern Book

by Rita Sova

This book was made with a little help from my friends:

Teresa Martinez (Bead Artist)
Jo Ann Roybal (Bead Artist)
Valerie Anaya (Bead Artist)
Nancy Rodriguez (Bead Artist)
Ann Mier (Bead Artist)
Karen Mertes (Editor)
Kay Bryant (Graphic Designer)

"Bead Pattern Designer" is the bead program I used for this and my
first two books, Thank you Mark Ramsey.

Thank you all!

This is a pattern book. Only basic technique instructions are provided.
There are many books on the market with technique instructions.
You can also check the internet.

I have provided the Delica bead numbers with some of the patterns; the color
description is my own. Please use the DB number when obtaining Delica Beads.
There are many colors available, please feel free to change to your own color choices.

I would love to see pictures of your work. You may contact me: Rita Sova
6121 Gibson Blvd SE (Mail only)
Albuquerque, NM 87108

Other Books by Rita Sova are:
Angel Design Book $ 24.95
Butterfly & Fairy Design Book $ 24.95

E-mail: Rita@twrol.com
Web site: www.BeadDesigns.com

Table of Contents

St. Therese Pouch

Beaded by Teresa Martinez

Terry is the one who prompted me to design this pouch and the large St. Therese Pattern also included in this book. Thanks Terry.

Delica Beads used by Terry Martinez:
DB 610 (S/L Violet-Flower)
DB 200 (Opaque White-Habit)
DB 42 (S/L Gold-Crown)
DB 205 (Ceylon Beige-Face)
DB 688 (S/L Green-Leaves)
DB 235 (Coral-Flower)
DB 734 (Opaque Brown-Cross)
DB 322 (Matte Metallic Gold-Cross)
DB 685 (S/L Dk Rose-Lips)
DB 310 (Matte Black-Habit)
DB 191 (Light Pink-Flower)
DB 785 (Dk Pink-Flower)
DB 81 (Lnd Dk Gray AB-Background)

Delica Beads used by Jo Ann Roybal:
DB 10 Hex (Black, Hex-Habit & Eyes)
DB 201 (White Pearl-Habit)
DB 42 Hex (S/L Gold, Hex-Crown)
DB 22 (Met Bronze-Crown)
DB 205 (Ceylon Beige-Face)
DB 984 (Lnd Mix, Green-Leaves)
DB 239 (Lt Aqua Pearl-Background)
DB 56 (Lnd Magenta AB-Flower)
DB 914 (Lnd Crystal Hot Pink-Flower)
DB 246 (Cotton Candy Pink Pearl-Flower)
DB 611 (S/L Wine-Cross)
DB 1 (Hematite-Cross)
DB 53 (Lnd Pale Yellow AB-Flower Centers)
DB 70 (Lnd Rose Pink AB-Lips)

Beaded by
Jo Ann Roybal
Santa Fe, NM 1999

St. Therese Pouch Pattern

Flat Peyote Stitch

Row 3:
Rows 1 & 2:

Start here:

Kokopelli Pouch
Flat Peyote Stitch

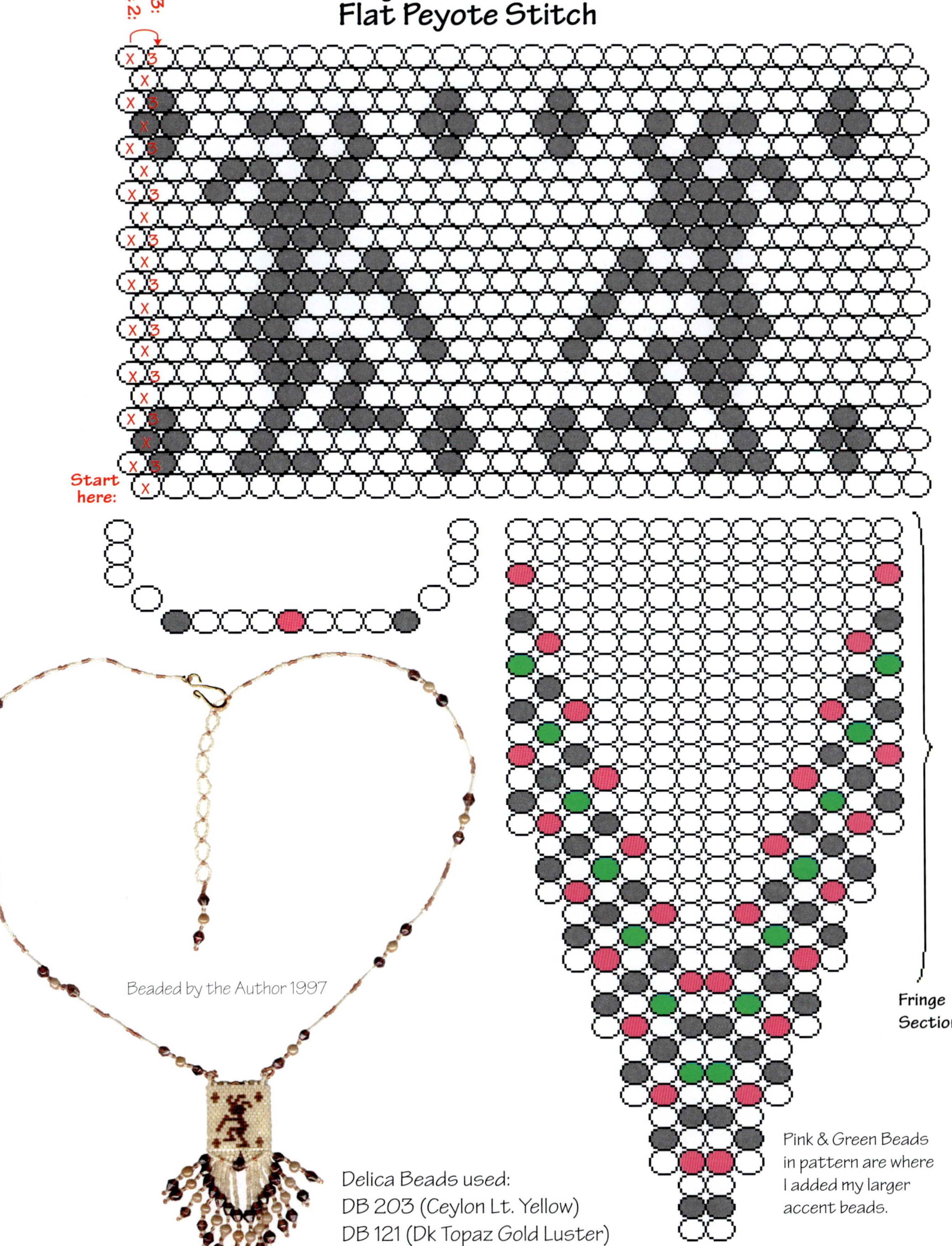

3

Kokopelli Earrings
Brick Stitch

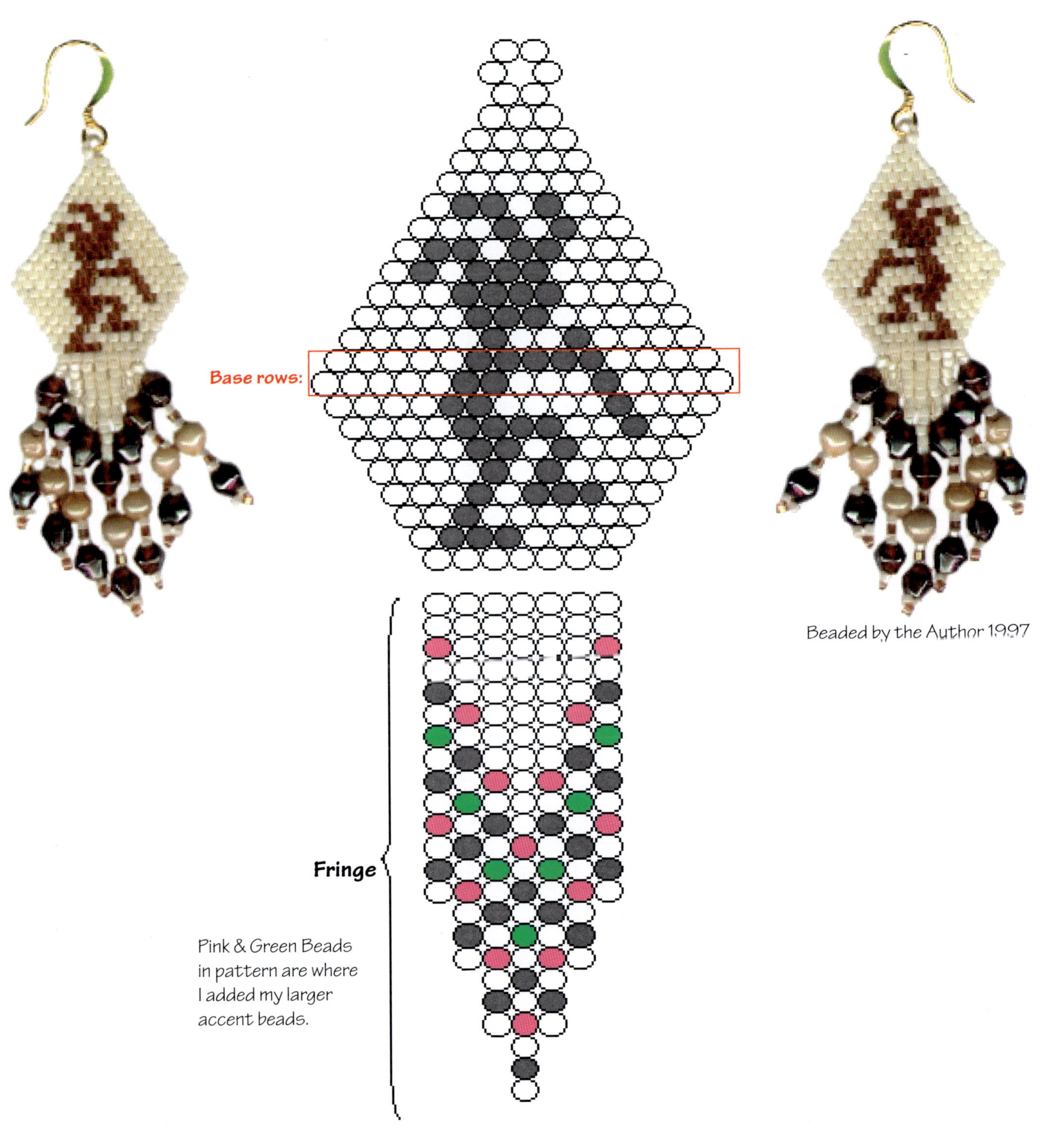

Our Lady of Guadalupe & Angel Pouch

Delica Beads used:
DB 211 (Alabaster)
DB 47 (S/L Sapphire)
DB 44 (S/L Lt Blue)
DB 35 (Galv. Silver)
DB 205 (Ceylon Beige)
DB 201 (White Pearl)
DB 10 (Black)
DB 362 (Matte Red)
DB 322 (Matte Metallic Gold)

Beaded by the Author 1998

Our Lady of Guadalupe & Angel
Pouch Pattern - Flat Peyote Stitch

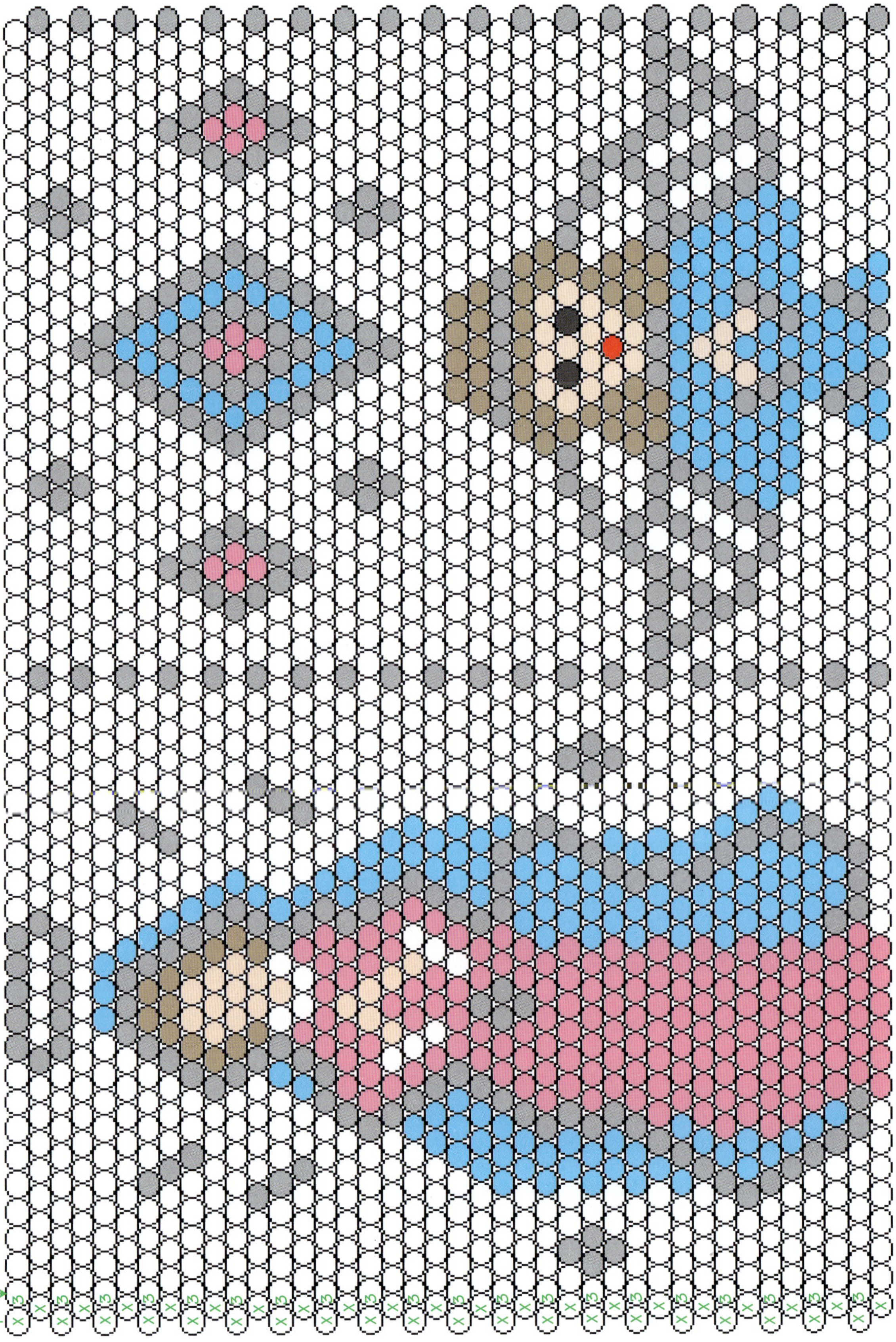

Our Lady of Guadalupe & Angel Pouch Fringe Idea

This fringe was designed for this double sided pouch. Notice there is a different design on each side.

Fringe Pattern: (23 fringe) Fringe hang only from the white beads. (white=background color bead)

Start from the left and work to the center then reverse for the opposite side.

Fringe #1 and 23:
Have thread\needle coming down out of the 1st white bead on the left side of the Angel side of pouch.
Pick up: 2 dk blue, 1 4mm Mother of Pearl (MOP), 3 dk blue, 8 white, 1-6mm lt blue and 6 silver.
Insert needle through 1st silver added and 1-6mm Lt blue and 1 white bead only.
Add 7 white, 2 dk blue, insert needle through 1 dk blue below MOP, MOP, and 1 dk blue above MOP.
Add 1 dk blue. Insert needle up into 1st white bead of pouch on Our Lady of Guadalupe (OLG)
side of pouch.
Adjust tension. Insert needle down out of the 2nd white bead on OLG side of pouch. Now you are ready
for fringe 2.

Fringe 2 & 22   OLG: 1 silver, 3 dk blue, MOP, 3 dk blue, 8 white, 1-6mm lt blue, 6 silver.
              Angel: 7 white, 2 dk blue, 2 dk blue, 1 silver.
Fringe 3 & 21:   Angel: 3 silver, 3 dk blue, MOP, 3 dk blue, 8 white, 1-6mm lt blue, 6 silver.
              OLG: 7 white, 2 dk blue, 2 dk blue, 3 silver.
Fringe 4 & 20: OLG: 5 silver, 3 dk blue, MOP, 3 dk blue, 8 white, 1-6mm lt blue, 6 silver.
              Angel: 7 white, 2 dk blue, 2 dk blue, 5 silver.
Fringe 5 & 19: Angel: 7 silver, 3 dk blue, MOP, 3 dk blue, 8 white, 1-6mm lt blue, 6 silver.
              OLG: 7 white, 2 dk blue, 2 dk blue, 7 silver.
Fringe 6 & 18: OLG: 2 white, 7 silver, 3 dk blue, MOP, 3 dk blue, 8 white, 1-6mm lt blue, 6 silver.
              Angel: 7 white, 2 dk blue, 2 dk blue, 7 silver, 2 white.
Fringe 7 & 17:   Angel: 4 white, 7 silver, 3 dk blue, MOP, 3 dk blue, 8 white, 1-6mm lt blue, 6 silver.
              OLG: 7 white, 2 dk blue, 2 dk blue, 7 silver, 4 white.
Fringe 8 & 16: OLG: 6 white, 7 silver, 3 dk blue, MOP, 3 dk blue, 8 white, 1-6mm lt blue, 6 silver.
              Angel: 7 white, 2 dk blue, 2 dk blue, 7 silver, 6 white.
Fringe 9 & 15: Angel: 8 dk blue, 7 silver, 3 dk blue, MOP, 3 dk blue, 8 white, 1-6mm lt blue, 6 silver.
              OLG: 7 white, 2 dk blue, 2 dk blue, 7 silver, 8 white.
Fringe 10 & 14: OLG: 10 white, 7 silver, 3 dk blue, MOP, 3 dk blue, 8 white, 1-6mm lt blue, 6 silver.
              Angel: 7 white, 2 dk blue, 2 dk blue, 7 silver, 10 dk blue.
Fringe 11 & 13: Angel: 1 dk blue, 1 silver, 10 dk blue, 7 silver, 3 dk blue, MOP, 3 dk blue, 8 white,
              1-6mm lt blue, 6 silver.
              OLG: 7 white, 2 dk blue, 2 dk blue, 7 silver, 12 white.
Fringe 12:   OLG: 14 white, 7 silver, 3 dk blue, MOP, 3 dk blue, 8 white, 1-6mm lt blue, 6 silver.
              Angel: 7 white, 2 dk blue, 2 dk blue, 7 silver, 10 dk blue, 4 silver.

The chain and top edge is your choice. Make it your own, be creative!

Our Lady of Guadalupe
Pin & Pattern

Beaded by the Author 1998

Brick Stitch

Delica Beads used:
DB 501 (Gold Iris)
DB 322 (Matte Metallic Gold)
DB 205 (Ceylon Beige)
DB 201 (White Pearl)
DB 607 (S/L Teal)
DB 78 (Lt Aqua)

Mini Flower Pouch & Earrings
Brick Stitch

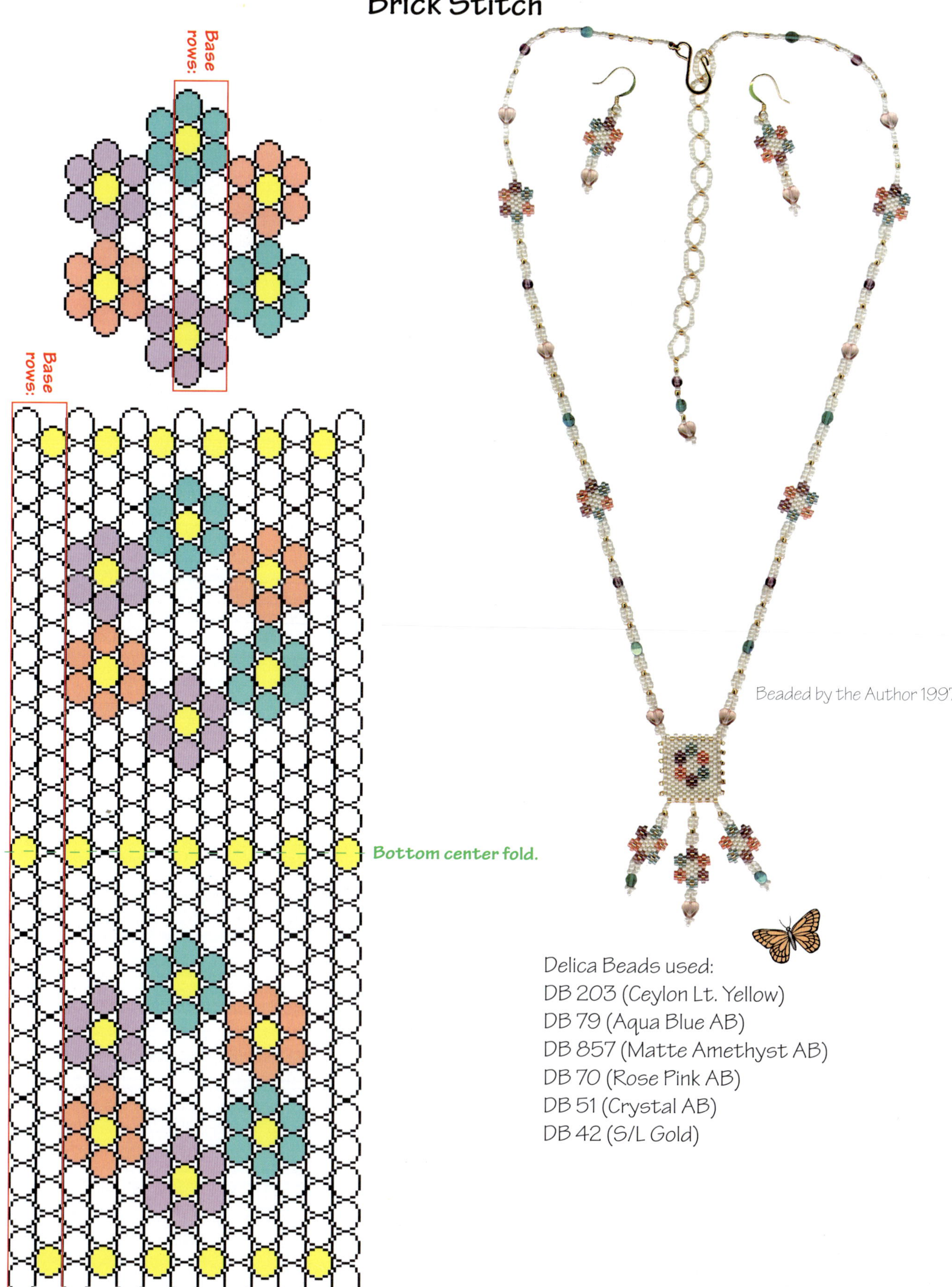

Delica Beads used:
DB 203 (Ceylon Lt. Yellow)
DB 79 (Aqua Blue AB)
DB 857 (Matte Amethyst AB)
DB 70 (Rose Pink AB)
DB 51 (Crystal AB)
DB 42 (S/L Gold)

Ladybug Earrings
Brick Stitch

Beaded by:
Valerie Anaya
Santa Fe, New Mexico 1999

Delica Beads used:
DB 723 (Opaque Red)
DB 654 (Dyed Opaque Cranberry)
DB 10 (Black)

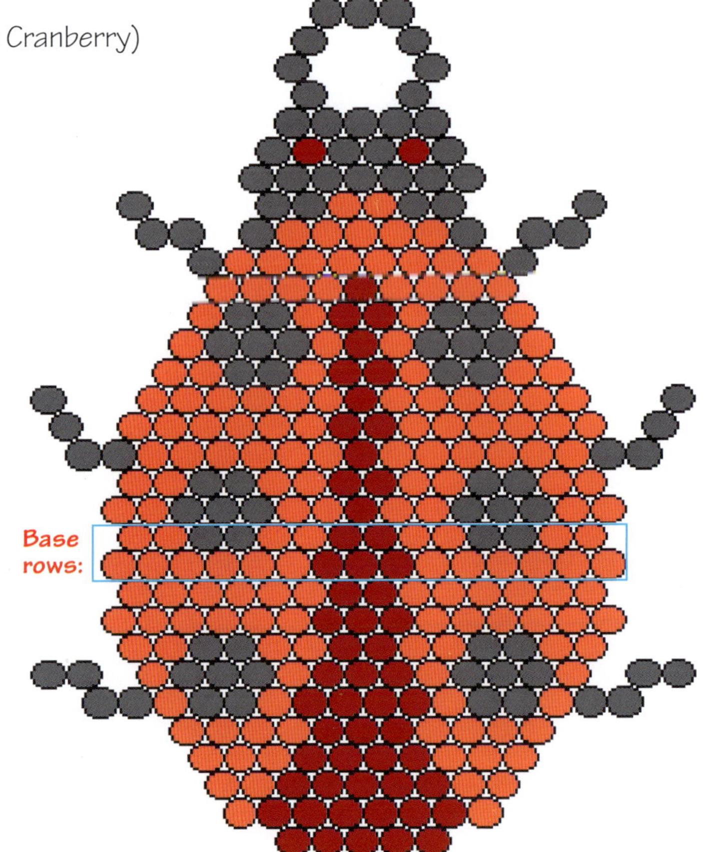

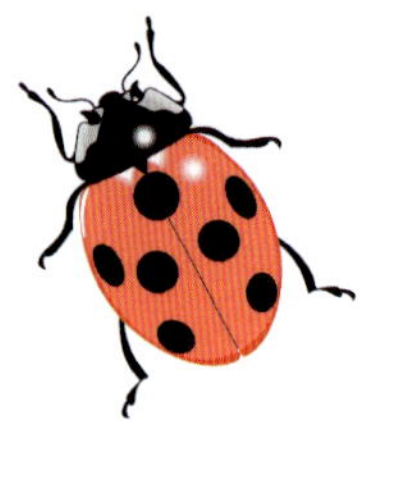

Ladybug Pouch

Delica Beads used:
DB 754 (Matte Opaque Pea Green)
DB 105 (Gold Luster Trsp Dk Red)
DB 378 (Brick Red)
DB 10 (Black)

Beaded by:
Teresa Martinez
Santa Fe, New Mexico 1999

Ladybug Pouch Pattern

Flat Peyote Stitch

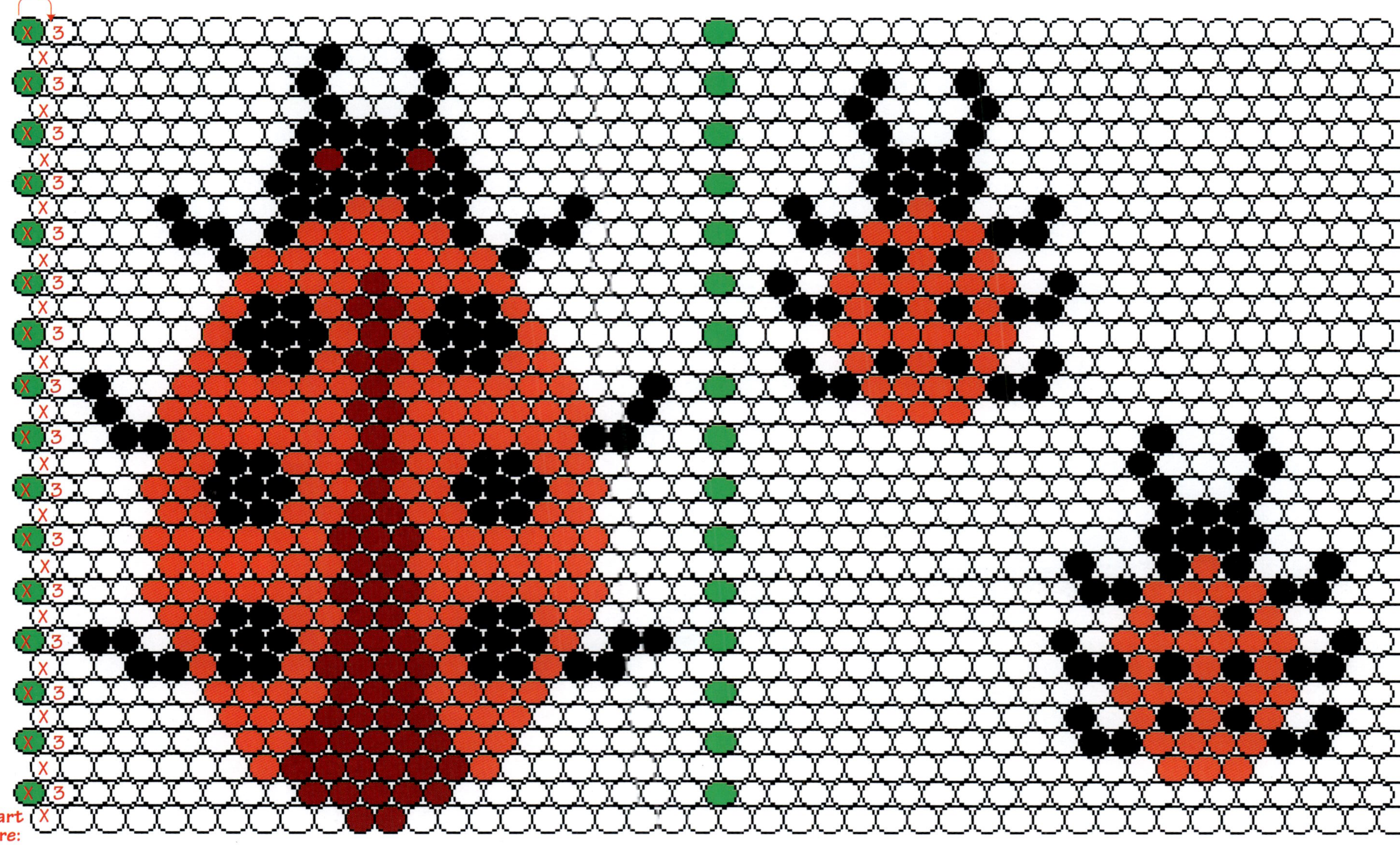

A Christmas Prayer Pouch
Flat Peyote Stitch

Delica Beads used:
DB 57 (Lnd Sky Blue AB)
DB 51 Hex (Crystal AB, Hex)
DB 201 (White Pearl)
DB 602 (S/L Red)
DB 205 (Ceylon Beige)
DB 42 (S/L Gold)
DB 696 (Semi-Matte S/L Cobalt, Eyes)
DB 362 (Matte Metallic Red AB)

A Christmas Prayer Pouch Pattern

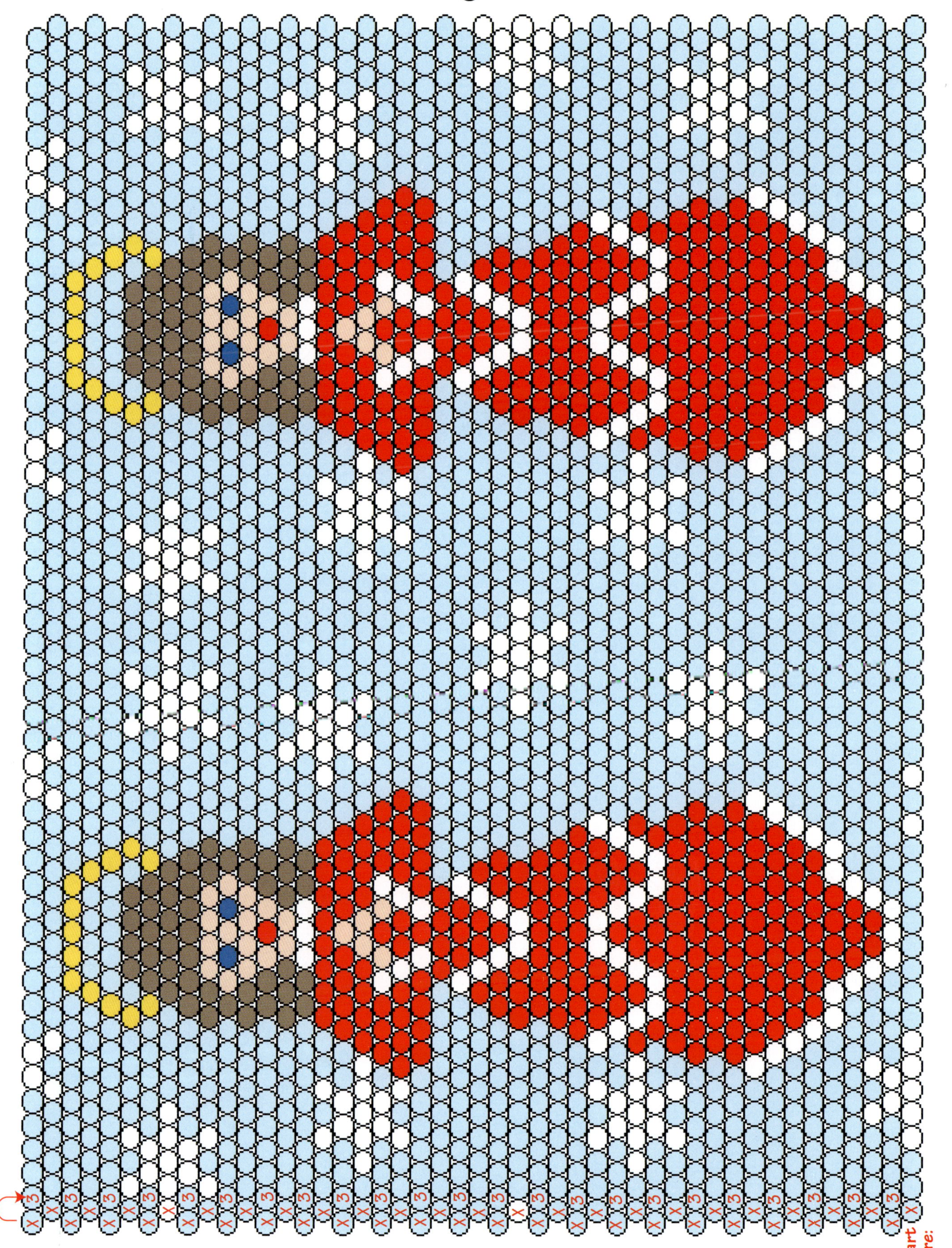

A Christmas Prayer Pin
Brick Stitch

Beaded by the Author 1999

Delica Beads used:
DB 602 (S/L Red)
DB 201 (White Pearl)
DB 612 (S/L Brown)
DB 105 (Red-Lip)
DB 10 (Black)
DB 205 (Ceylon Beige)

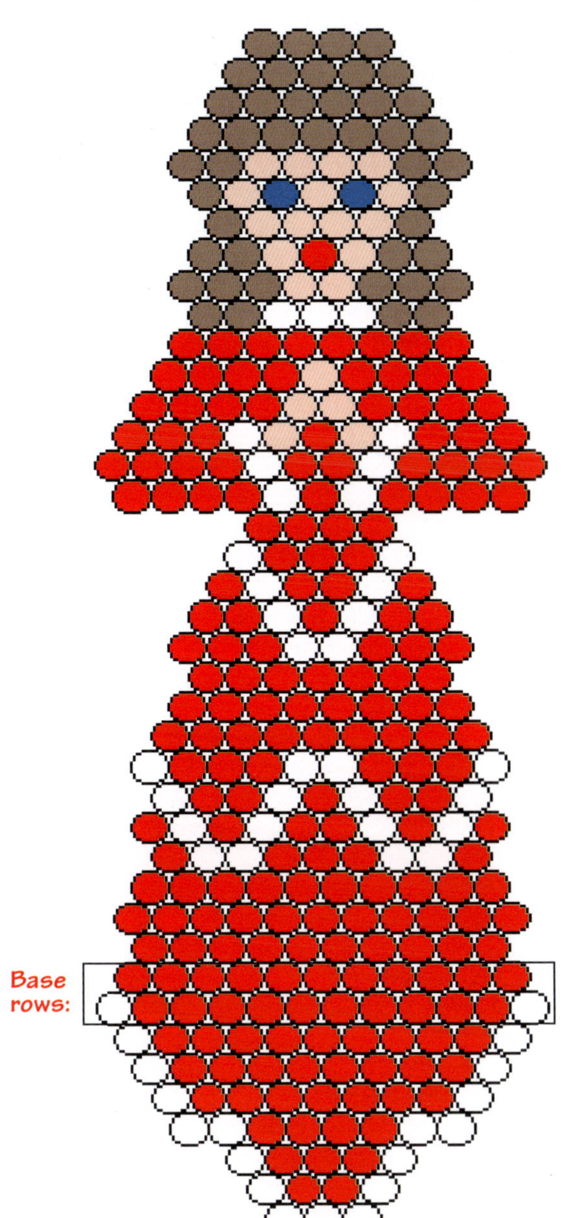

Hair Sticks

Flat Peyote Stitch

Designs using Delica Beads and 3/16" hair stick

Beaded by the Author 1999

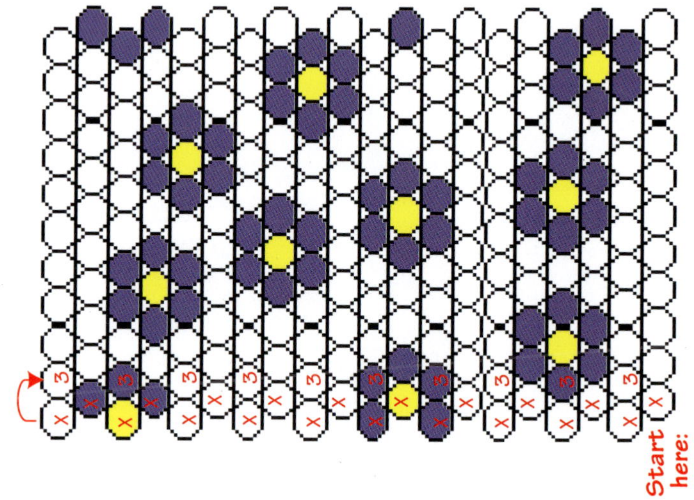

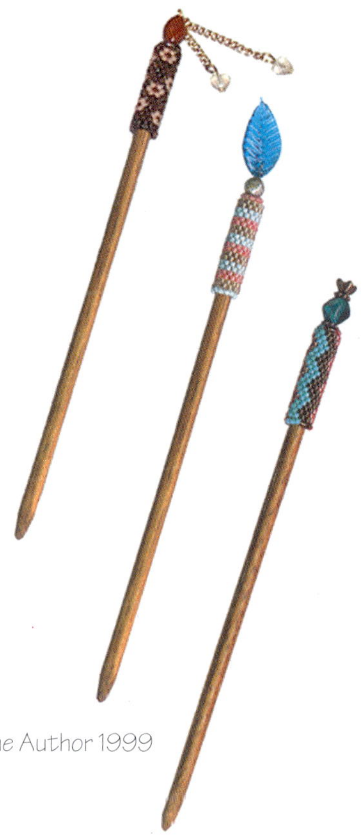

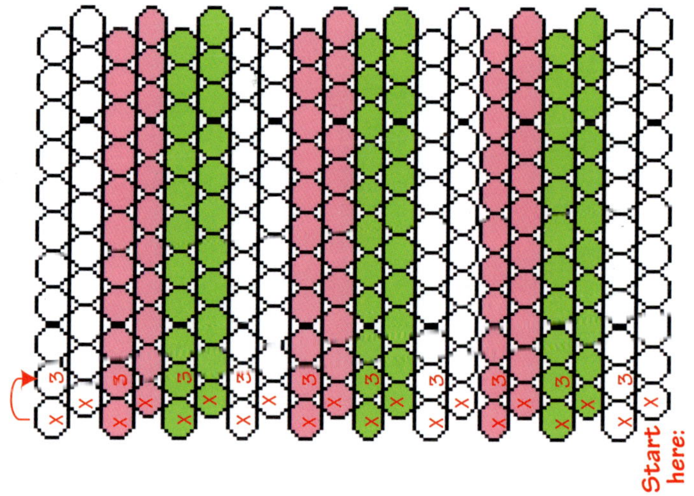

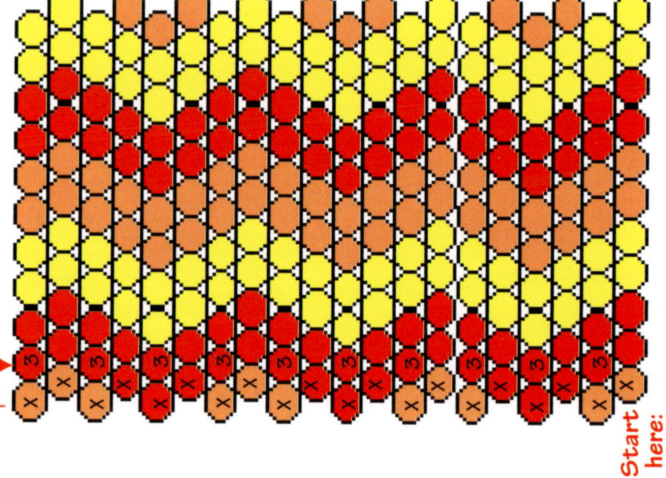

You can make your own hair sticks by purchasing 3/16" dowels and cutting them approximately 6-1/2" in length. Use a pencil sharpener or knife to get a dull point on the ends. I also used a wood stain on these.

To add adornments on the top: I drilled a tiny hole to accommodate the eye pin I used, then glued in the eye pin after adding my desired fringe/dangles.

Have fun.

Hair Sticks
Flat Peyote Stitch
Designs using Delica Beads and 3/16" hair stick

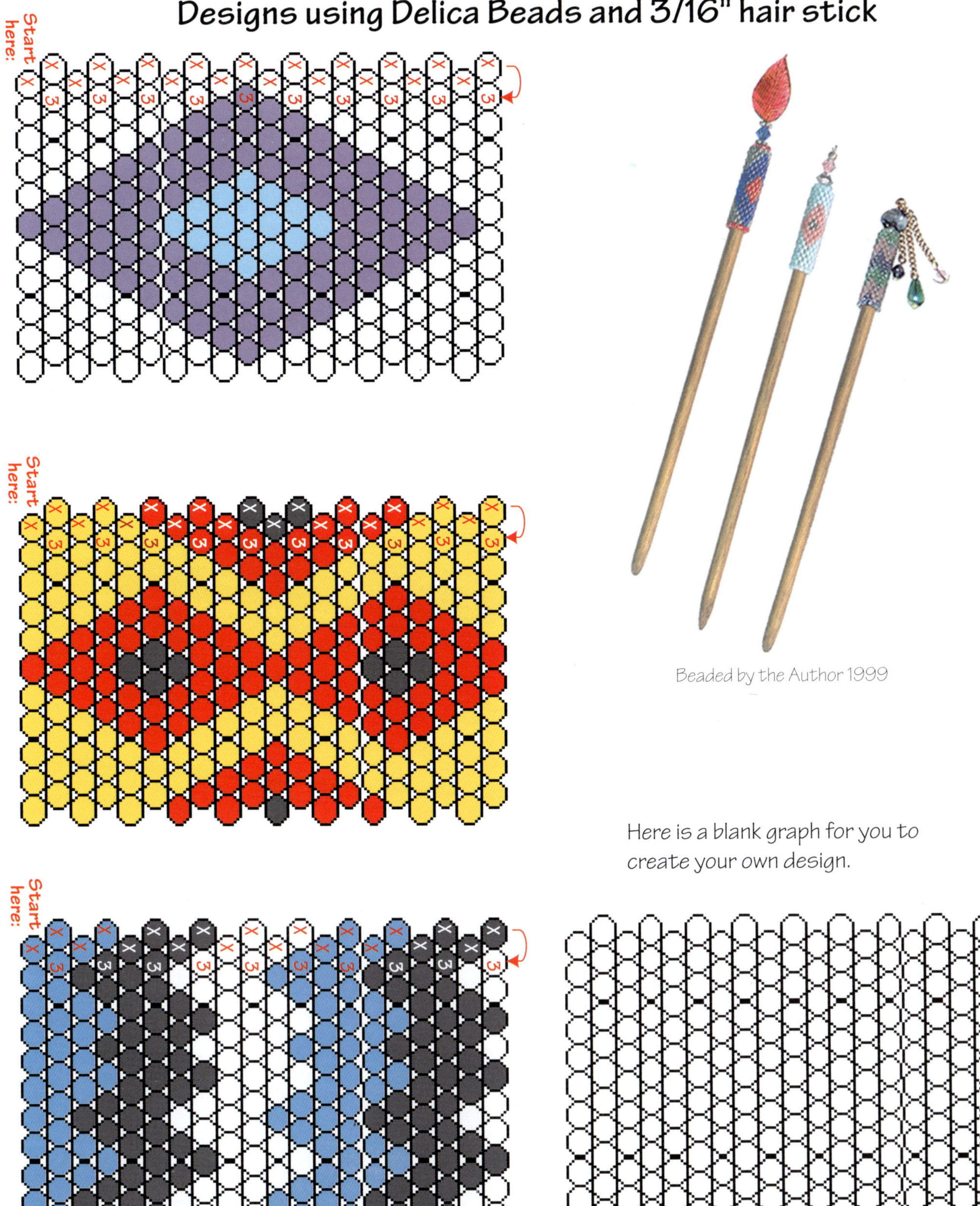

Ghost Earrings
Brick Stitch

Beaded by:
Top Center: Rita Sova, Albuquerque, NM 1997
Bottom: Valerie Anaya, Santa Fe, NM 1999

Delica Beads used by Rita:
DB 51 (Crystal AB)
DB 10 (Black)
Delica Beads used by Valerie:
DB 201 (Pearl White)
DB 10 (Black)

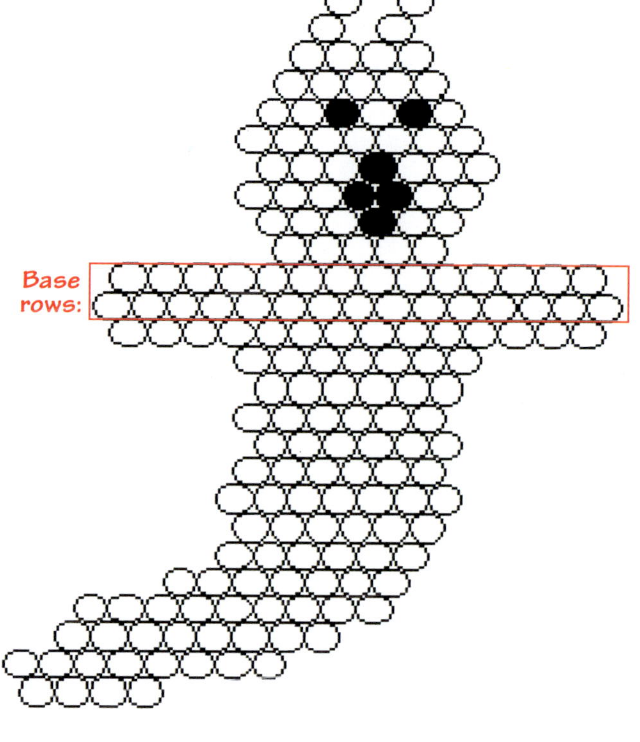

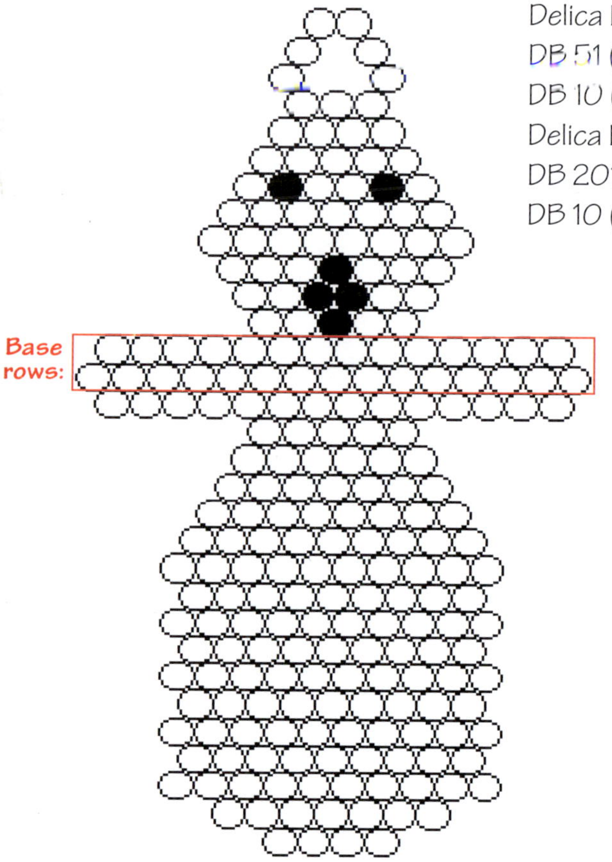

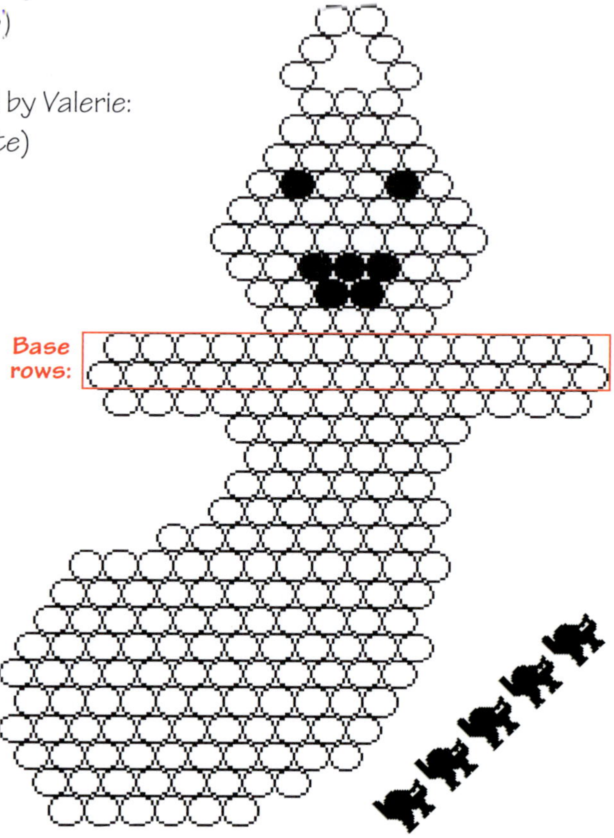

Heart Earrings
Brick Stitch & Fringe

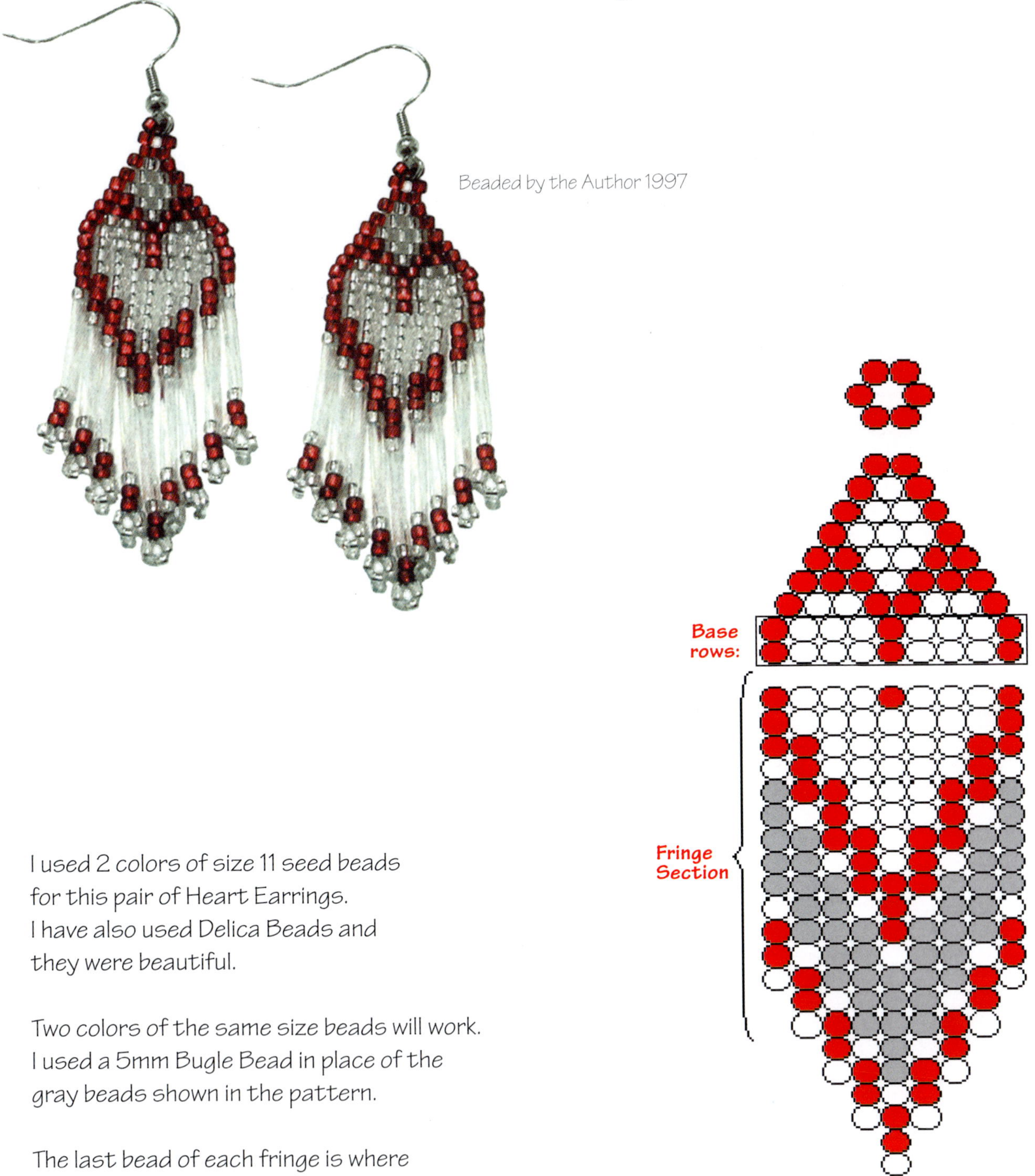

I used 2 colors of size 11 seed beads
for this pair of Heart Earrings.
I have also used Delica Beads and
they were beautiful.

Two colors of the same size beads will work.
I used a 5mm Bugle Bead in place of the
gray beads shown in the pattern.

The last bead of each fringe is where
you will add your turn around beads.
I like a 5 or 7 bead turn around. You
should do what you want, they are your
earrings.

Heart Pin

Brick Stitch

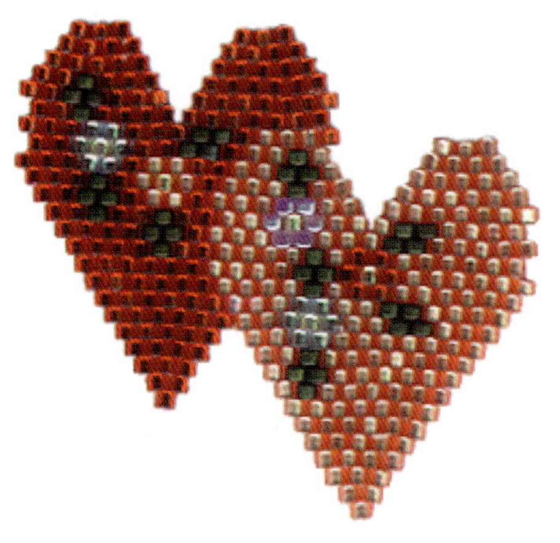

Beaded by the Author 1999

Delica Beads used:
DB 602 (S/L Red)
DB 684 (S/L Semi Matte Pink)
DB 42 (S/L Gold)
DB 327 (Matte Green)
DB 44 (S/L Blue)
DB 249 (Lt Violet Pearl)

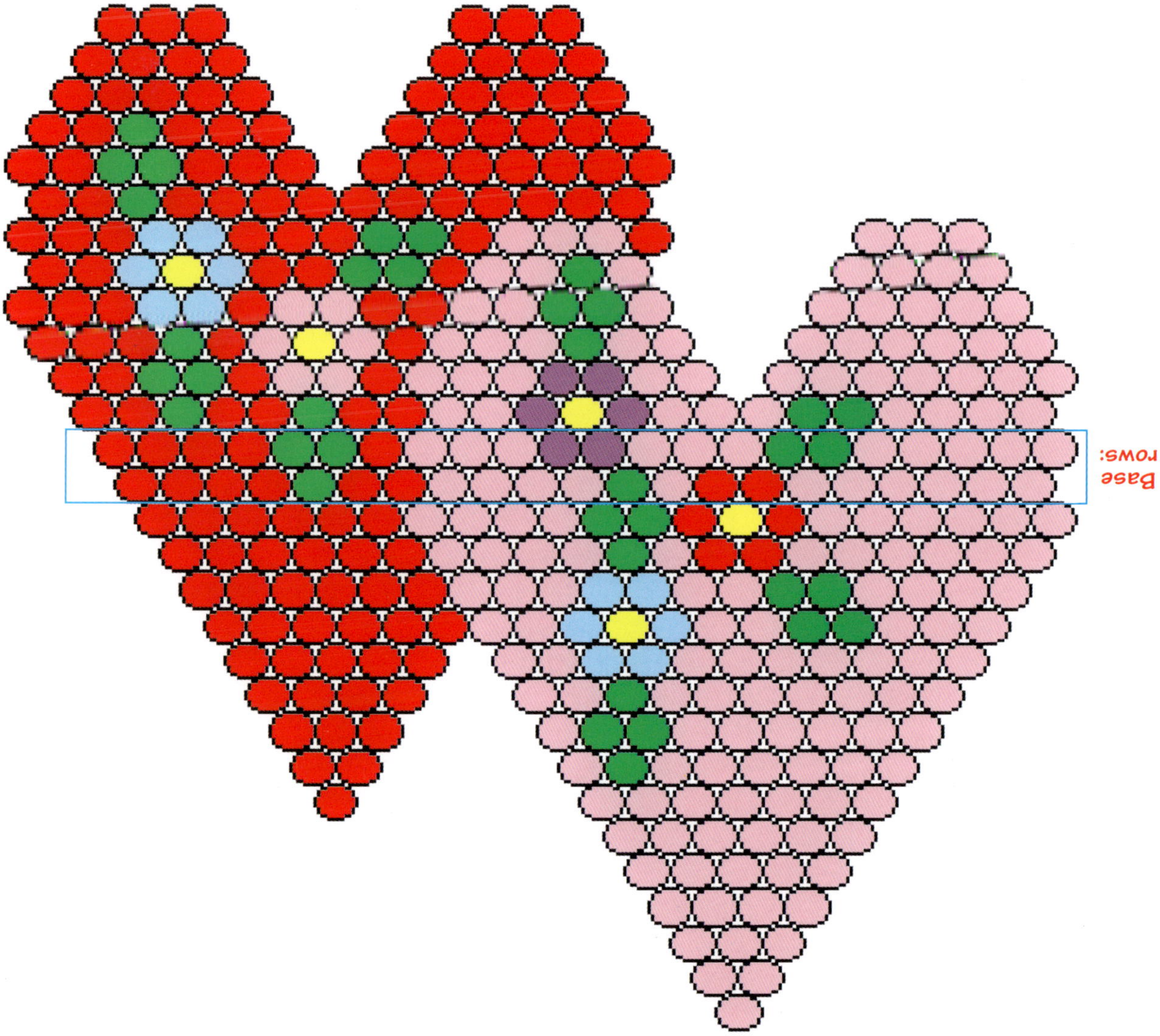

Rocking Horse Pin
Brick Stitch

Delica Beads used:
DB 272 (Lnd Topaz/Yellow AB)
DB 252 (Ceylon Gray)
DB 723 (Opaque Red)
DB 10 (Black)

Beaded by the Author 1997

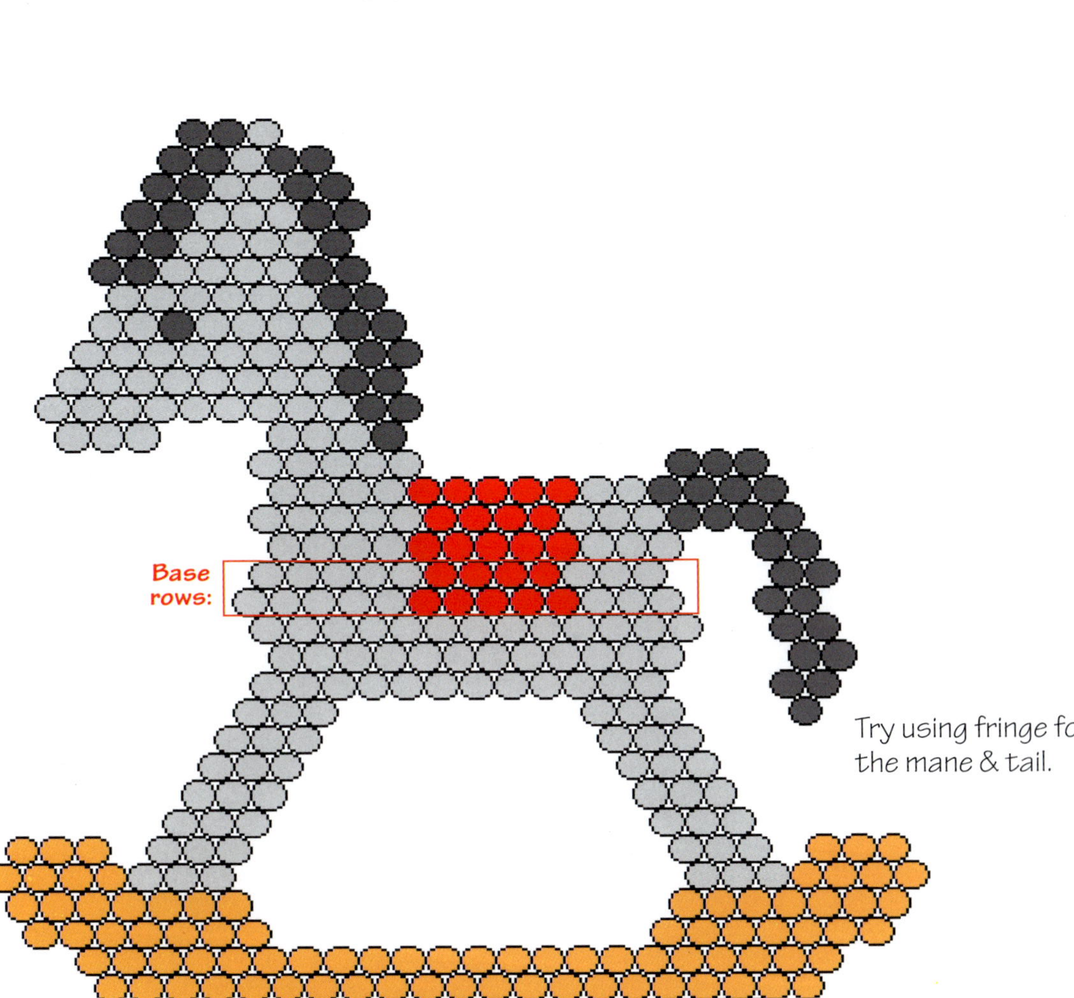

8 Ball Pin & Earrings

Brick Stitch

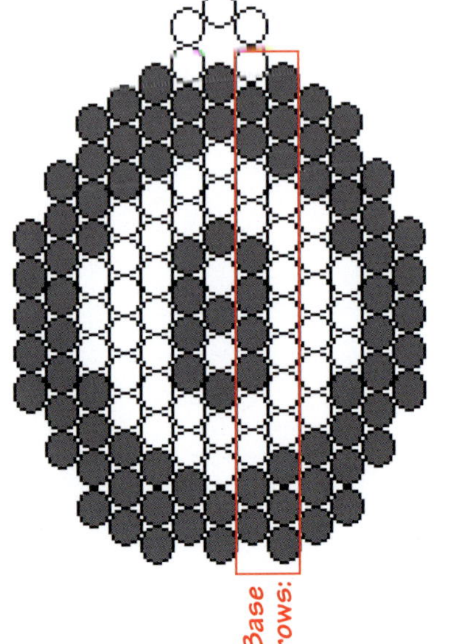

Beaded by the Author 1997

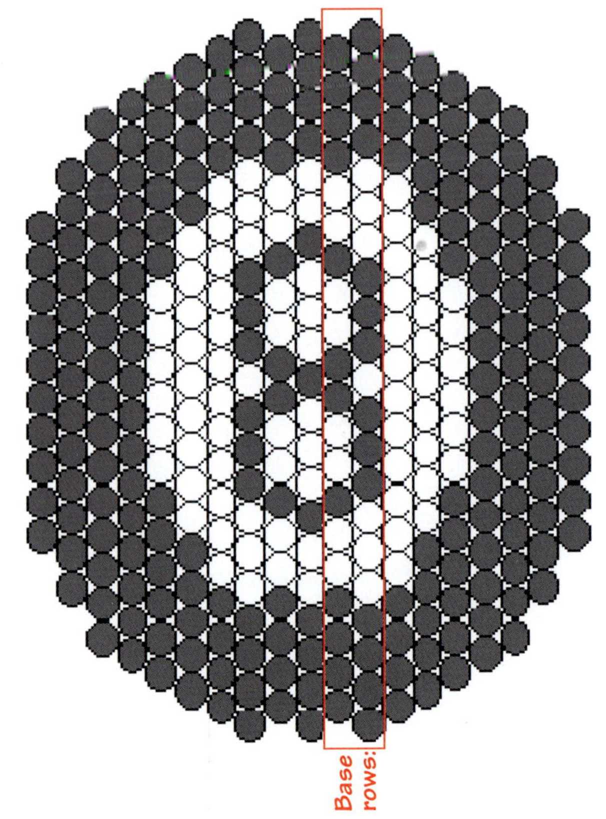

Beaded by the Author 1997

Delica Beads used:
DB 200 (Opaque White)
DB 10 (Black)

Another request by Teresa Martinez. Her husband plays pool and now the team has 8-Ball pins.

Balloon Pins

*Brick Stitch for the Balloon
Square for the Basket*

Moon & Stars

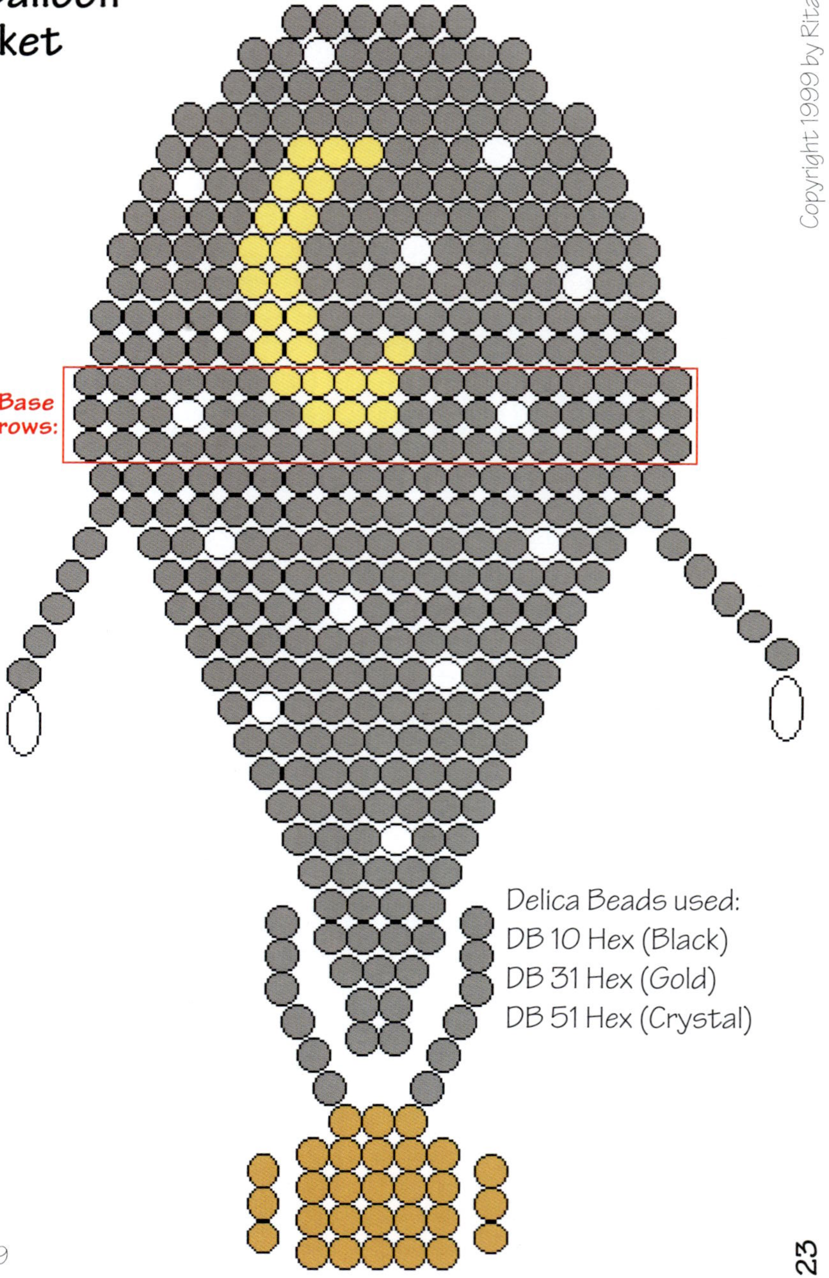

Delica Beads used:
DB 10 Hex (Black)
DB 31 Hex (Gold)
DB 51 Hex (Crystal)

Base rows:

Beaded by the Author 1999

Geo 1

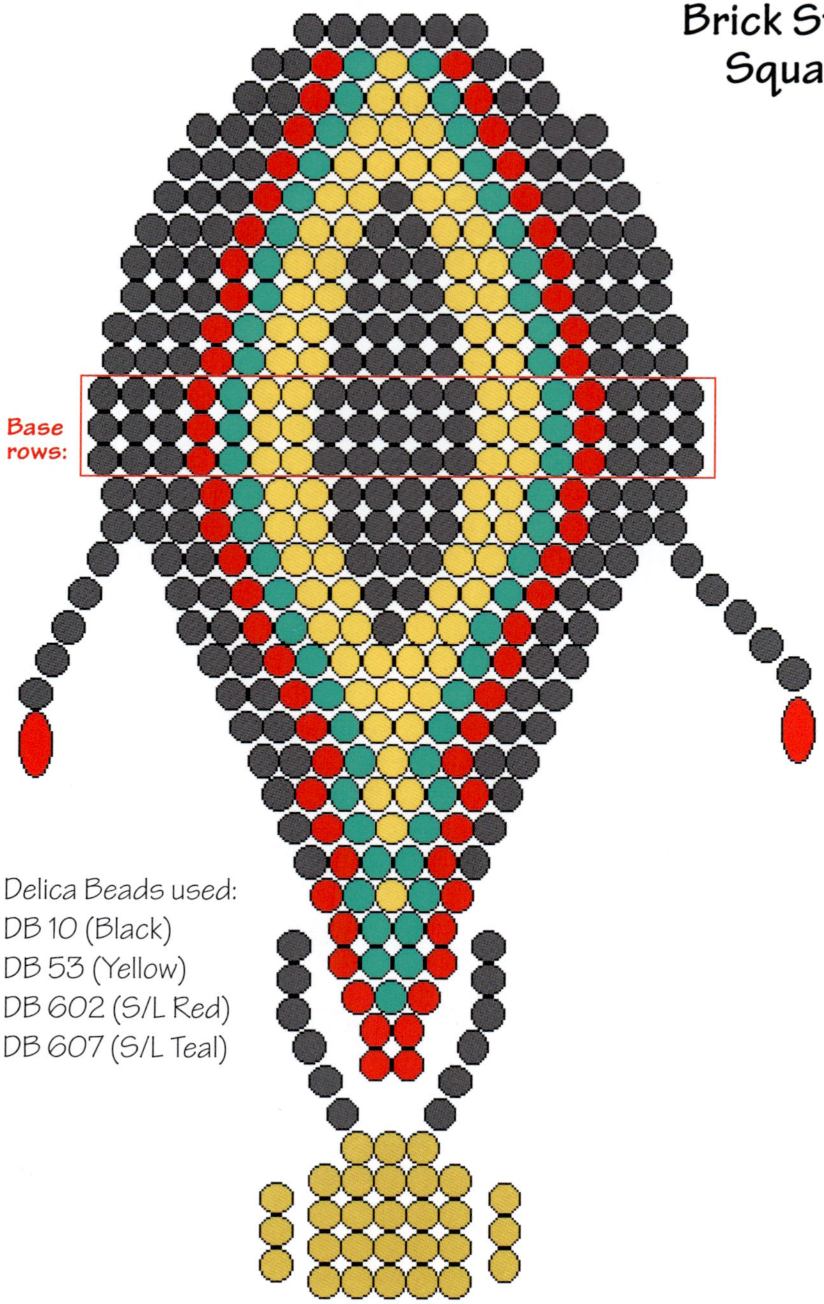

Delica Beads used:
DB 10 (Black)
DB 53 (Yellow)
DB 602 (S/L Red)
DB 607 (S/L Teal)

Base rows:

Balloon Pins

Brick Stitch for the Balloon
Square for the Basket

Sunset

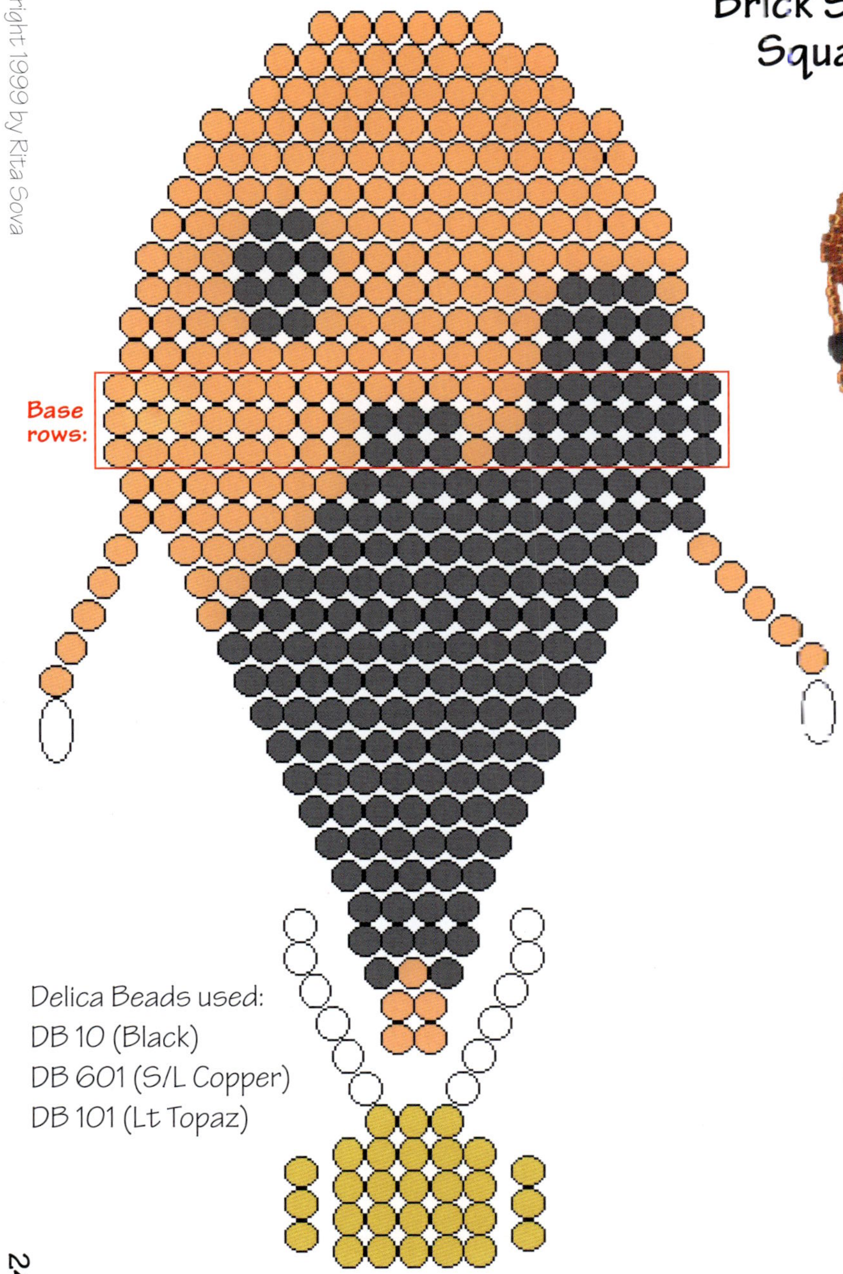
Base rows:

Delica Beads used:
DB 10 (Black)
DB 601 (S/L Copper)
DB 101 (Lt Topaz)

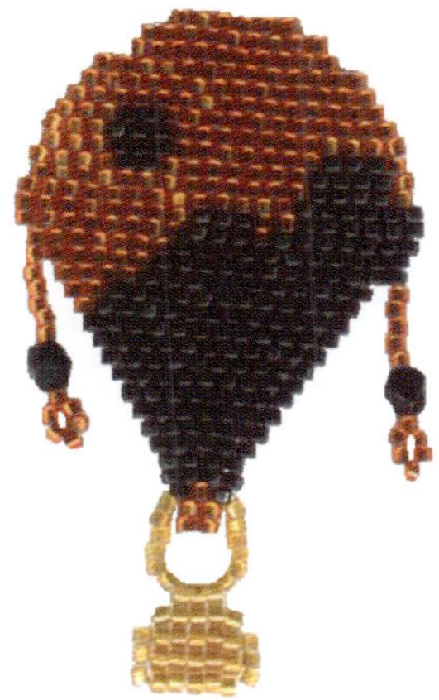

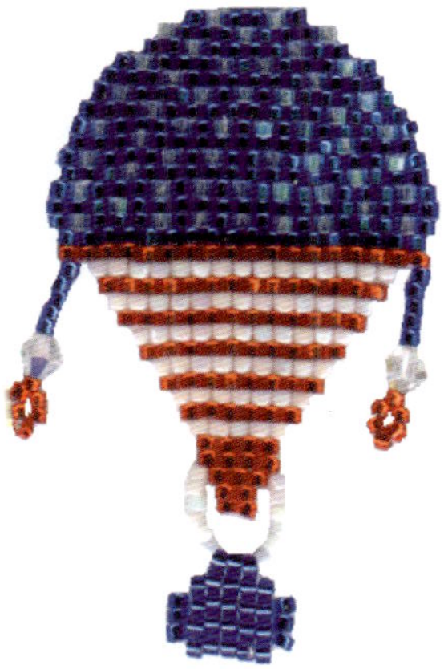

Beaded by the Author 1999

Flag

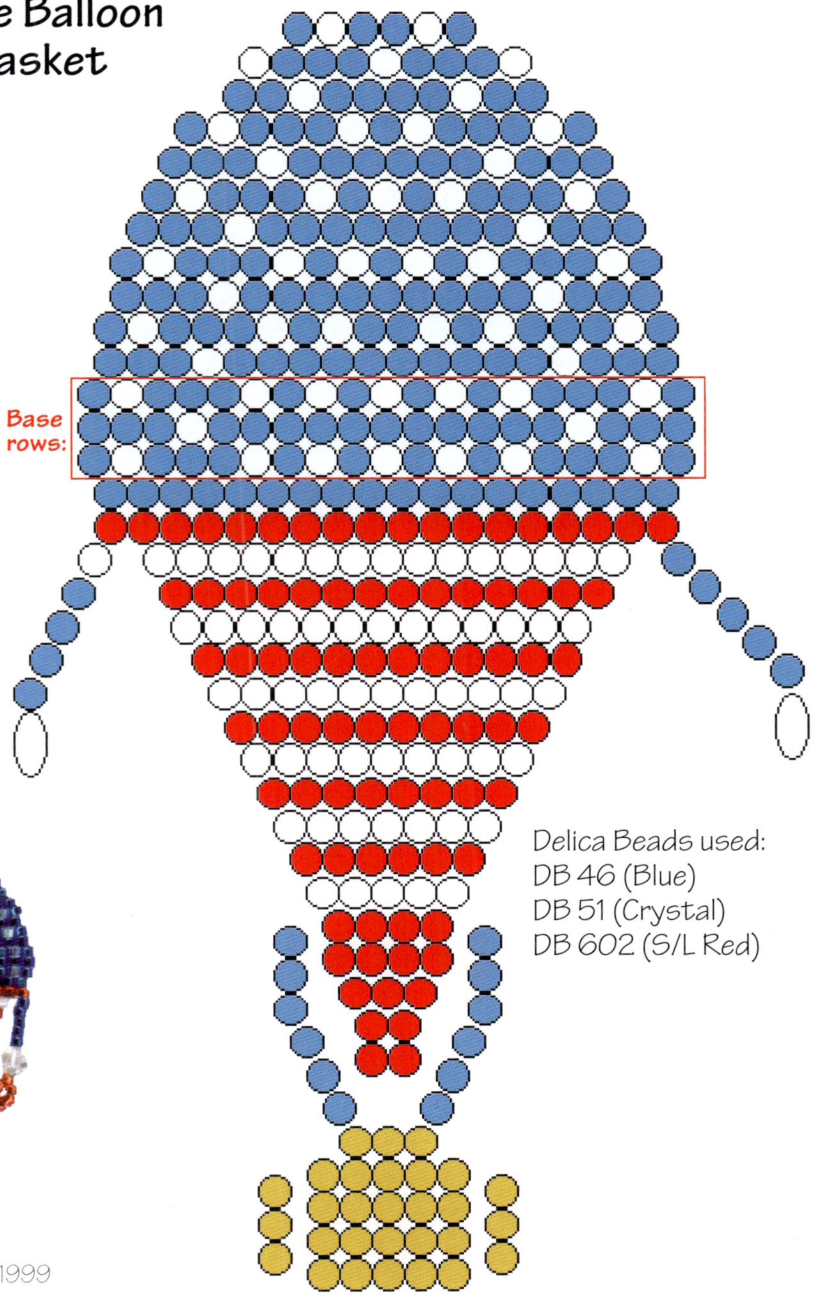
Base rows:

Delica Beads used:
DB 46 (Blue)
DB 51 (Crystal)
DB 602 (S/L Red)

Spiral

Balloon Pins

**Brick Stitch for the Balloon
Square for the Basket**

Flag 2

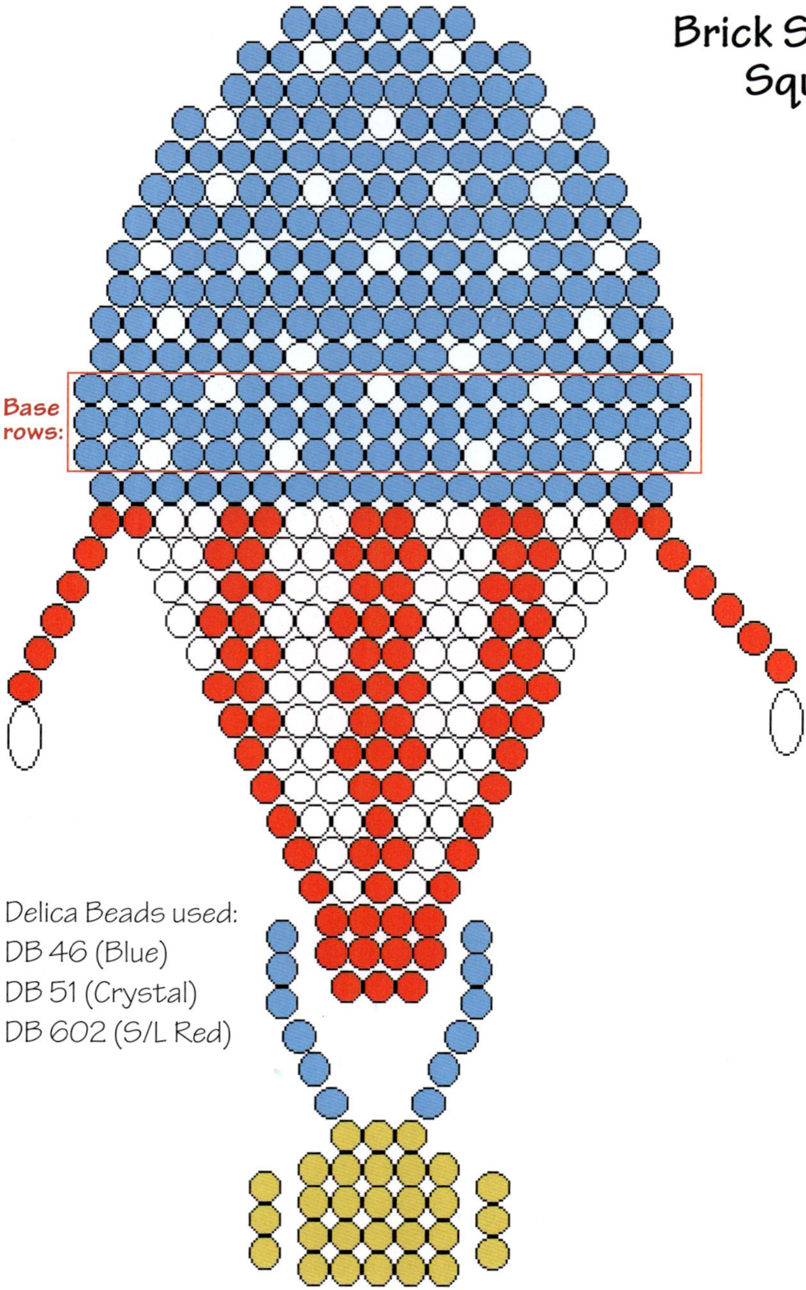

Base rows:

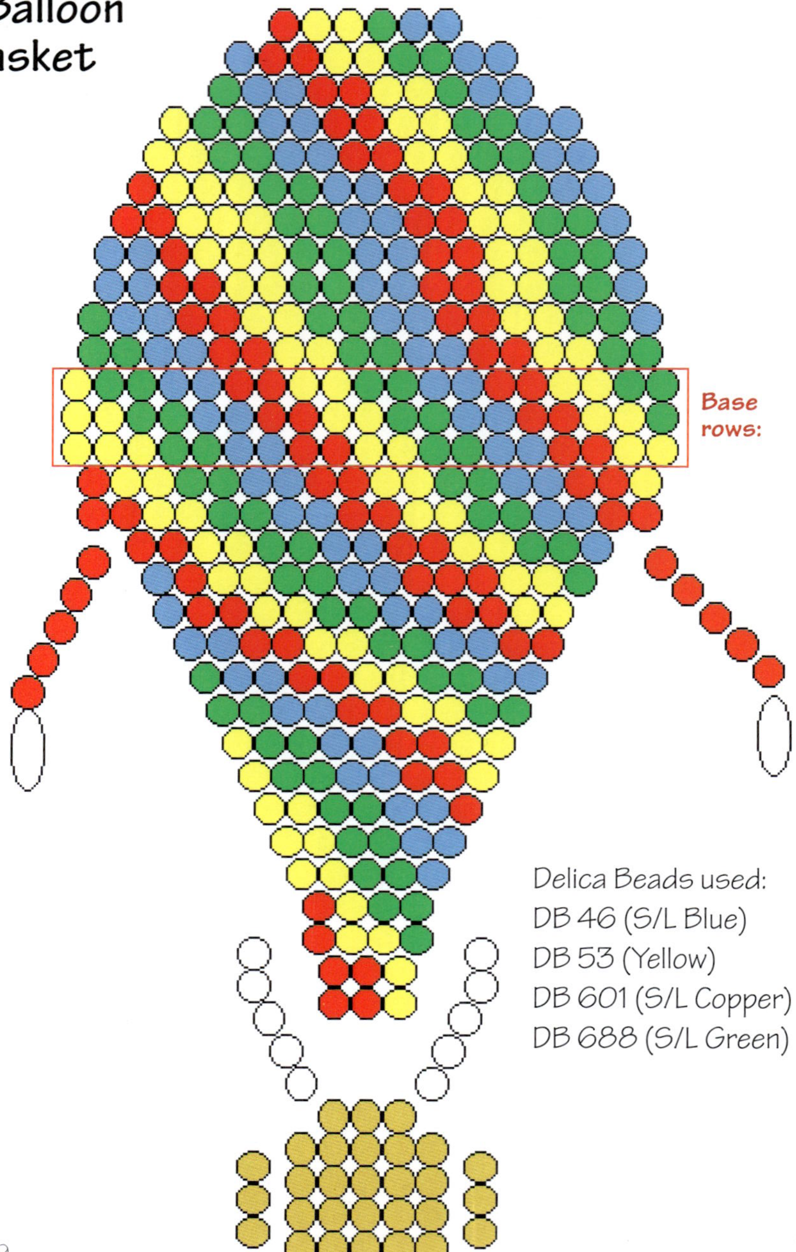

Delica Beads used:
DB 46 (S/L Blue)
DB 53 (Yellow)
DB 601 (S/L Copper)
DB 688 (S/L Green)

Beaded by the Author 1999

Delica Beads used:
DB 46 (Blue)
DB 51 (Crystal)
DB 602 (S/L Red)

Balloon Pins

Brick Stitch for the Balloon
Square for the Basket

Vertical Stripes

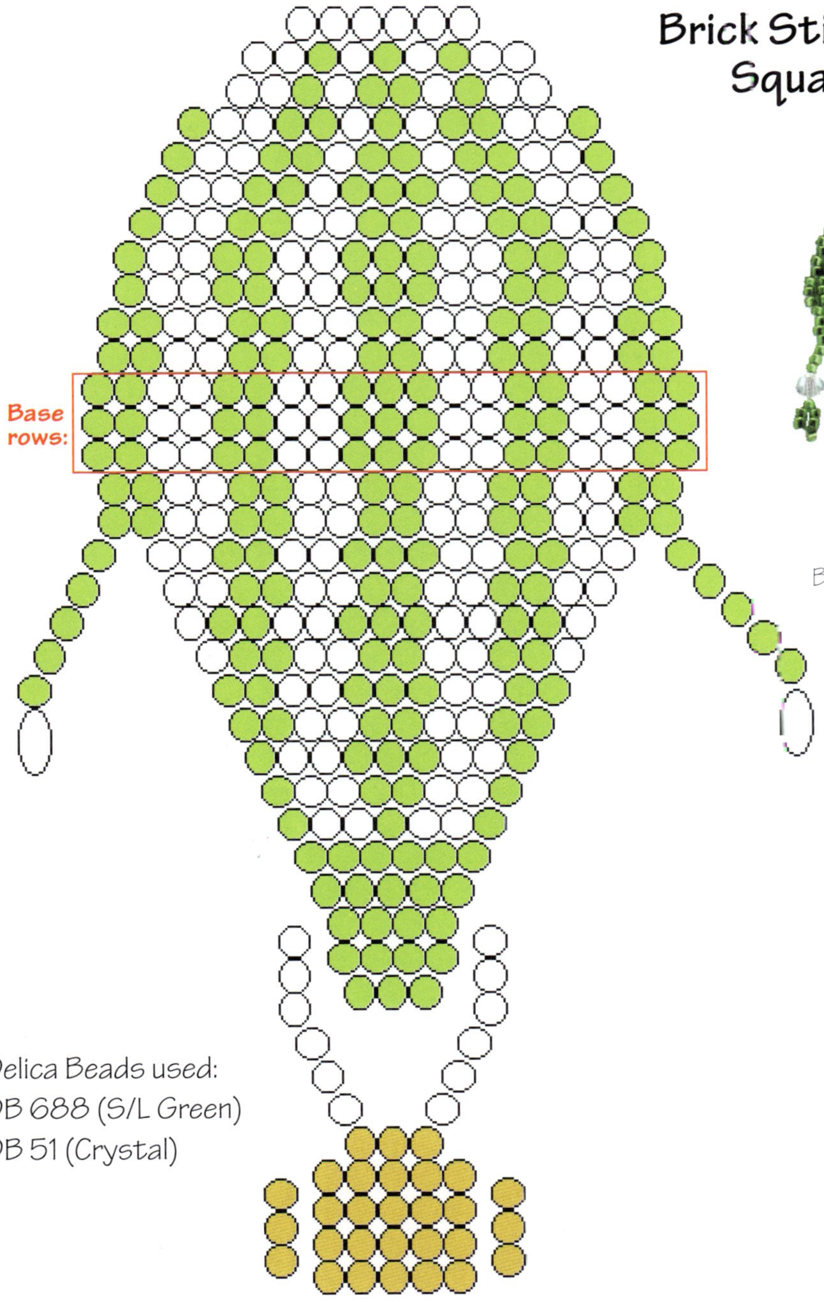

Design Your Own

Base rows:

Beaded by the Author 1999

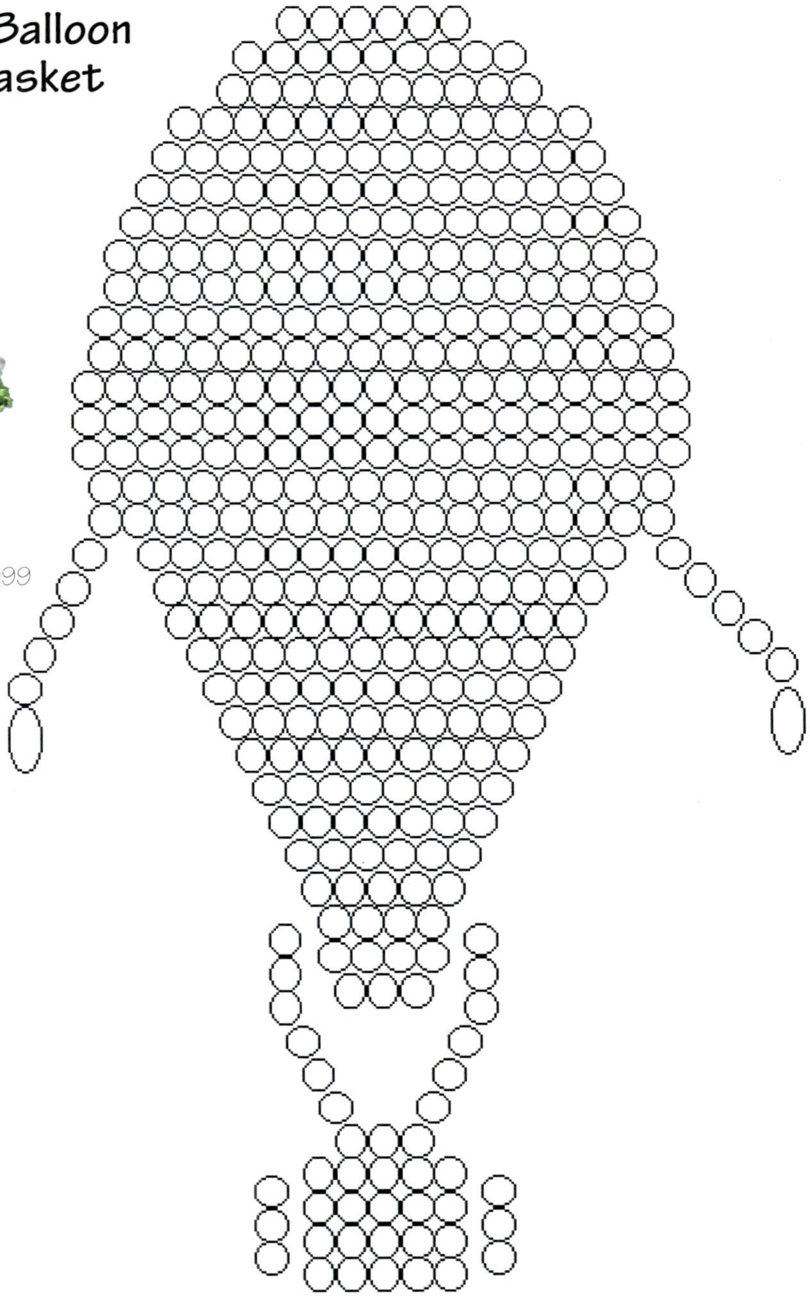

Delica Beads used:
DB 688 (S/L Green)
DB 51 (Crystal)

Balloon Pouch - Night & Day
Flat Peyote Stitch
October Skies in Albuquerque

Delica Beads used:
DB 10 (Black)
DB 50 (Crystal Luster)
DB 684 (S/L Rose)
DB 53 (Yellow)
DB 160 (Opaque Yellow)
DB 612 (S/L Brown)
DB 907 (Shimmering Sand)
DB 274 (Lnd Green/Lime)
DB 35 (Galvanized Silver)
DB 688 (S/L Med.Green)
DB 694 (S/L Purple)
DB 414 (Galvanized Aqua)
DB 31 (22 Kt. Gold)
DB 77 (Lnd Blue AB)
DB 57 (Lnd Sky Blue AB)
DB 741 (Matte Trsp Crystal)

**New Mexico is the
"Land of Enchantment".**

I mixed 2 shades of blue to
get the effect shown for the
Day Balloon Pouch.

Beaded by the Author 1998-99

Balloon Pouch - Night & Day

Flat Peyote Stitch

Row 3:
Rows 1 & 2:

Start here rows 1 & 2:

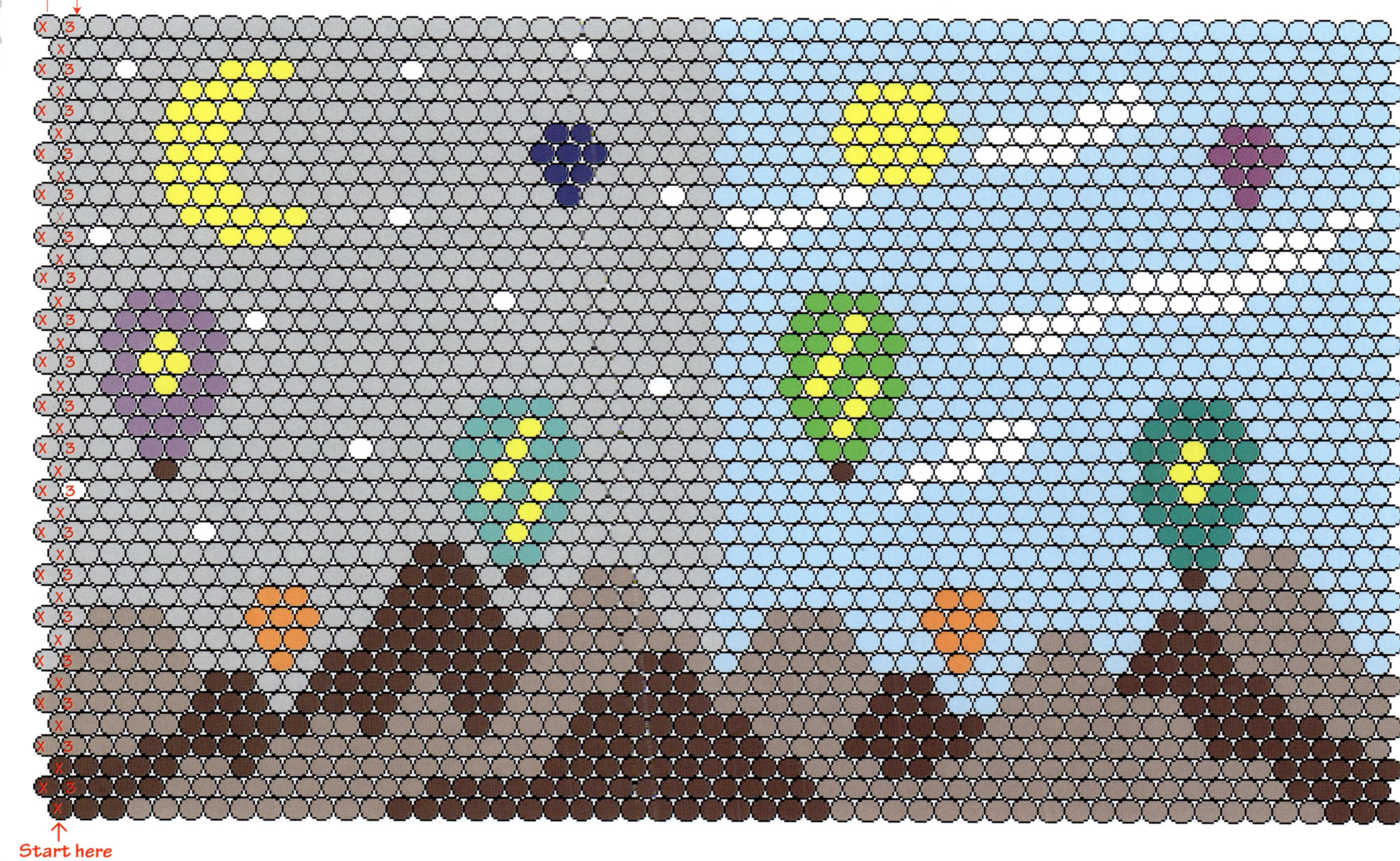

Monarch Butterfly Earrings
Brick Stitch

Delica Beads used:
DB 10 (Black)
DB 41 (S/L Crystal)
DB 681 (S/L Squash)

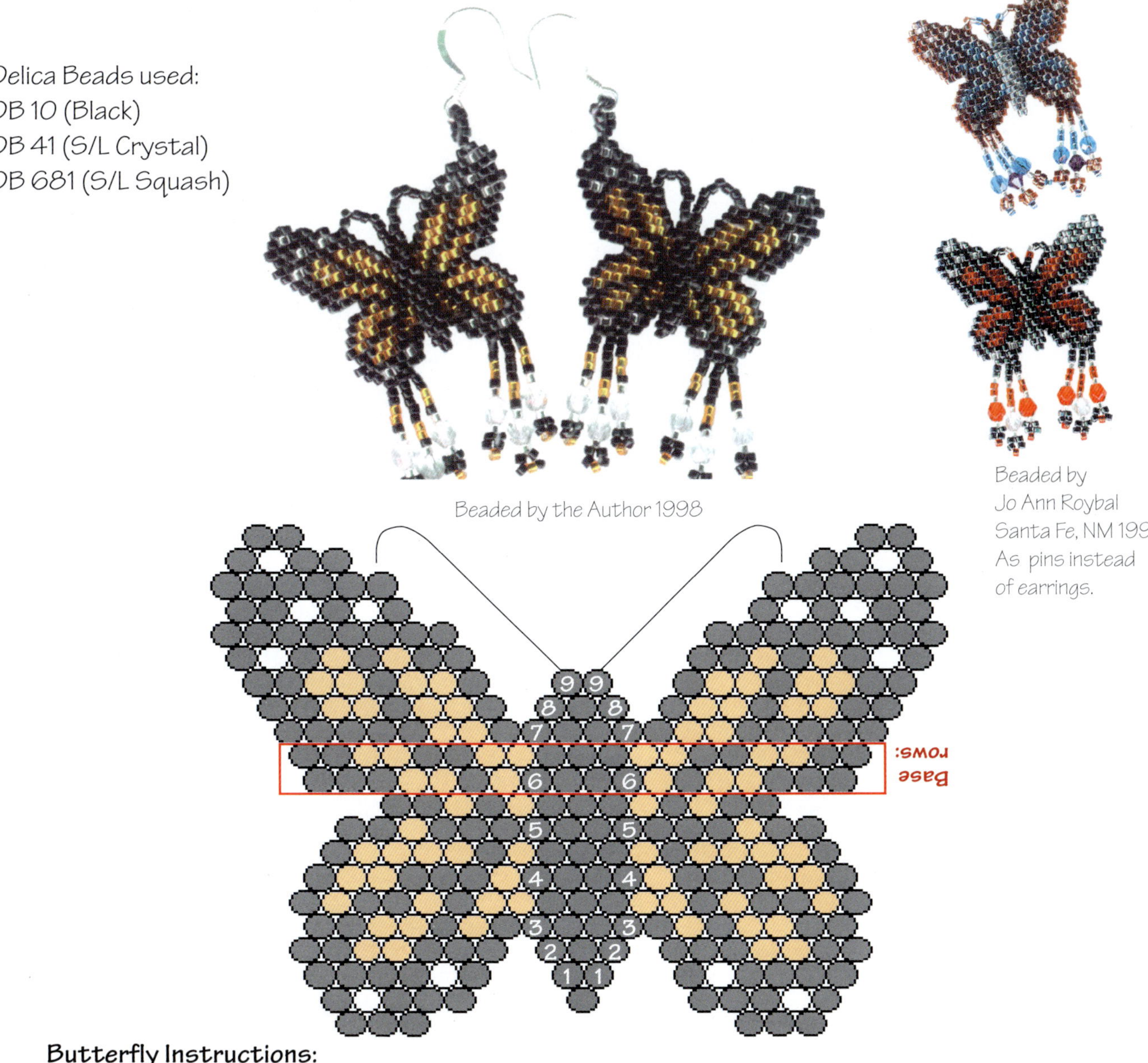

Butterfly Instructions:

1. Brick stitch the pattern as shown (1 piece).
2. Body/head/tail must be shaped. Fold body in half; pinch wings together at body to make body rounded.
3. Start at one of the number 1 beads. Circle stitch it to the other number 1 bead.
4. Circle stitch the number 2 beads together.
5. Repeat up the body circle stitching the matching numbered beads together.
6. At the top you may add antennae. I use thread (not wire) 3 - 4 threads through each antenna.
7. Fringe is your option. I added 1 to each of the bottom wing beads. (3 on each wing)
8. Attach to desired medium. For earrings I added a top loop of beads to add the ear wire.

Sometimes clear nail polish is needed to stiffen the wings. Always try a test spot first.

Butterfly Earrings
Shaded

Brick Stitch

Beaded by the Author 1999

Delica Beads used:
DB 2 (Blue Iris)
DB 57 (Lnd Sky Blue AB)
DB 41 (S/L Crystal)
DB 239 (Lt Aqua Pearl)

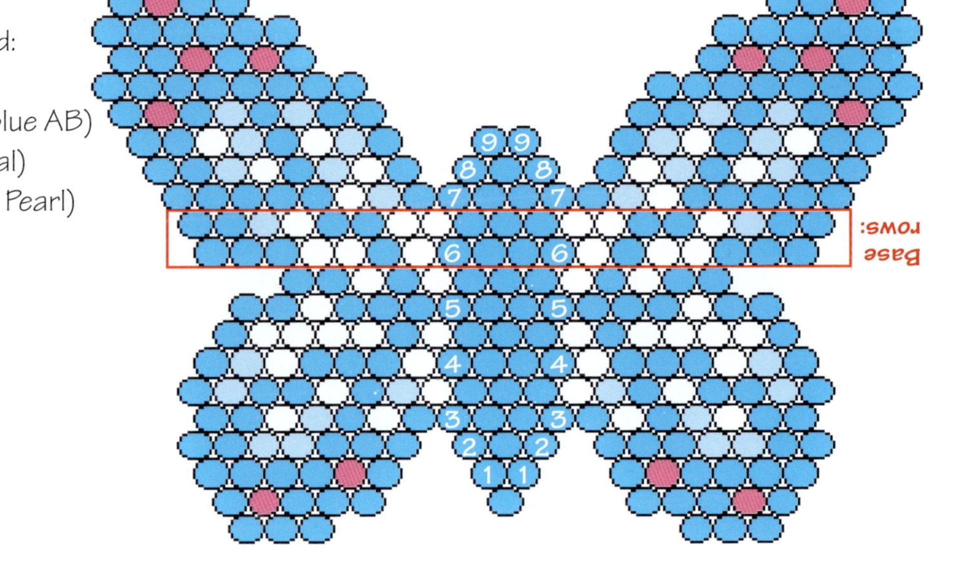

Beaded by Jo Ann Roybal
Santa Fe, NM 1999
As pins instead of earrings.

Butterfly Earrings
Painted

Brick Stitch

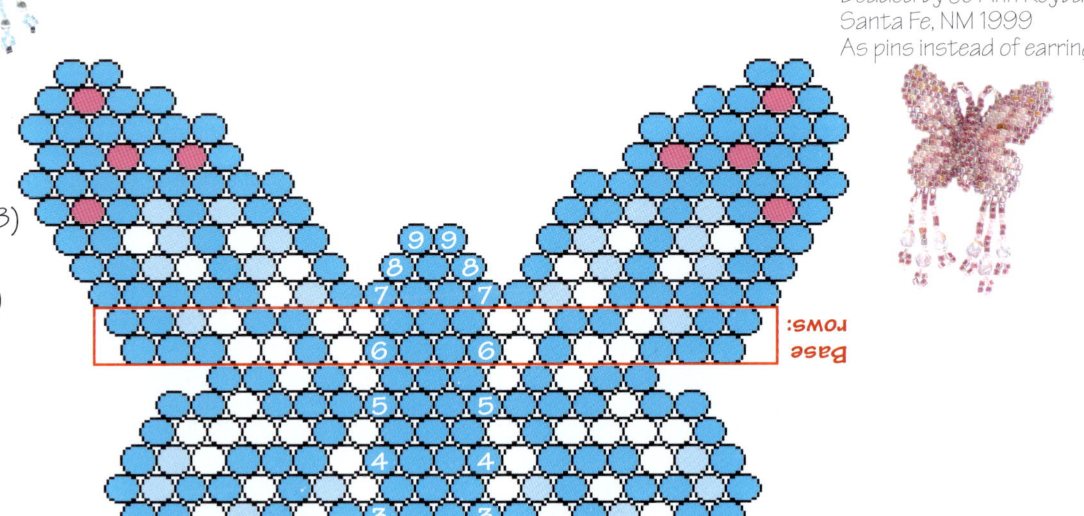

Beaded by:
Nancy Rodriguez
Santa Fe, NM 1999

Delica Beads used:
DB 162 (Opaque Red AB)
DB 76 (Lnd Lt. Blue AB)
DB 55 (Lnd Pale Pink AB)
DB 42 (S/L Gold)

Butterfly Pin (Medium)
Monarch
Brick Stitch

Delica Beads used:
DB 607 (S/L Teal)
DB 238 (Lnd Crystal Green Aqua Luster)
DB 41 (S/L Crystal)

Butterfly Instructions:

1. Brick stitch the pattern as shown (1 piece).
2. Body/head/tail must be shaped. Fold body in half; pinch wings together at body to make body rounded.
3. Start at one of the number 1 beads. Circle stitch it to the other number 1 bead.
4. Circle stitch the number 2 beads together.
5. Repeat up the body circle stitching the matching numbered beads together.
6. At the top you may add antennae. I use thread (not wire) 3 - 4 threads through each antenna.
7. Fringe is your option.
8. Attach to desired medium.

Sometimes clear nail polish is needed to stiffen the wings. Always try a test spot first.

Butterfly Pin (Medium) Shaded

Brick Stitch

Delica Beads used:
- DB 62 (Lnd Strawberry Ice AB)
- DB 162 (Opaque Red AB)
- DB 203 (Ceylon Lt. Yellow)
- DB 697 (Semi-Matte S/L Gray)

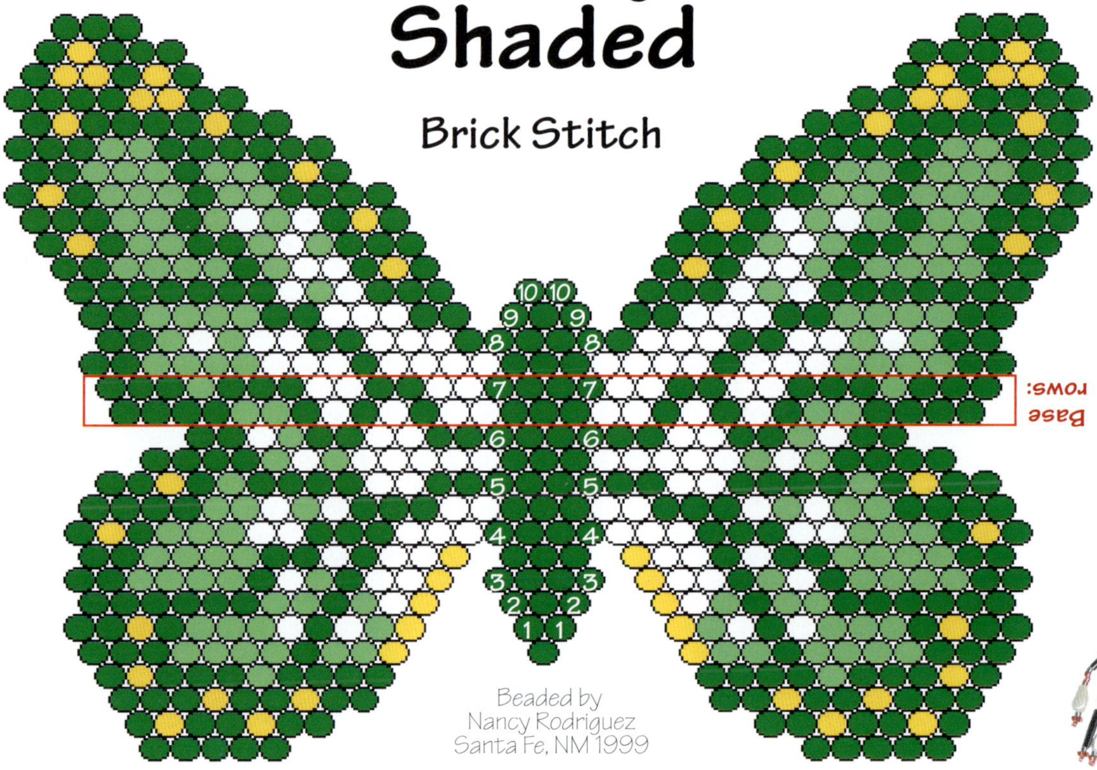

Base rows:
1 2 3 4 5 6 7 8 9 10

Beaded by
Nancy Rodriguez
Santa Fe, NM 1999

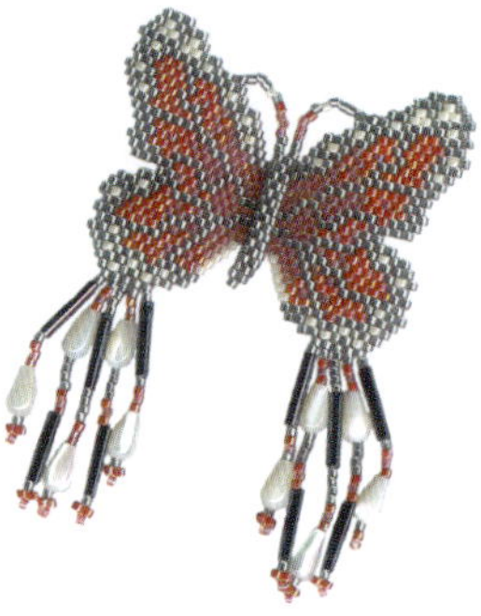

Beaded by the Author 1999

Butterfly Pin (Medium) Painted

Brick Stitch

Delica Beads used:
- DB 1 (Purple Iris)
- DB 42 (S/L Gold)
- DB 201 (White Pearl)
- DB 914 (Lnd Hot Pink)

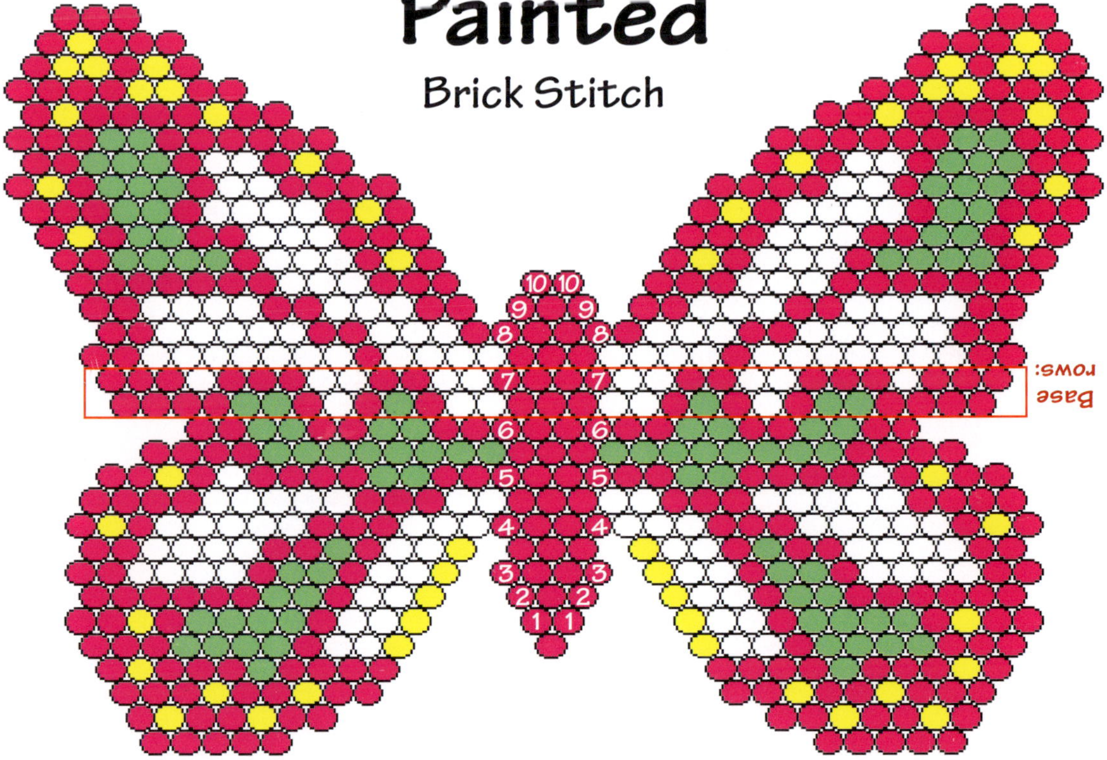

Base rows:
1 2 3 4 5 6 7 8 9 10

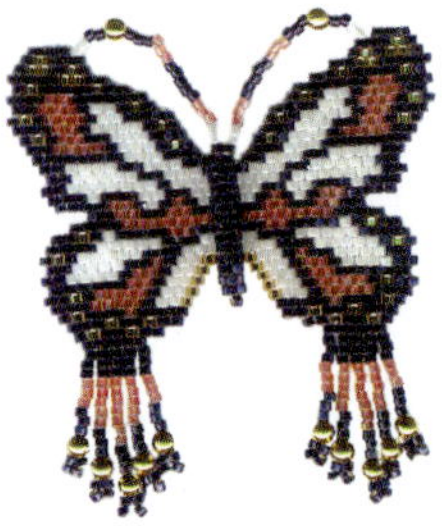

Beaded by
Nancy Rodriguez,
Santa Fe, NM 1999

Butterfly, Large Shaded
Brick Stitch

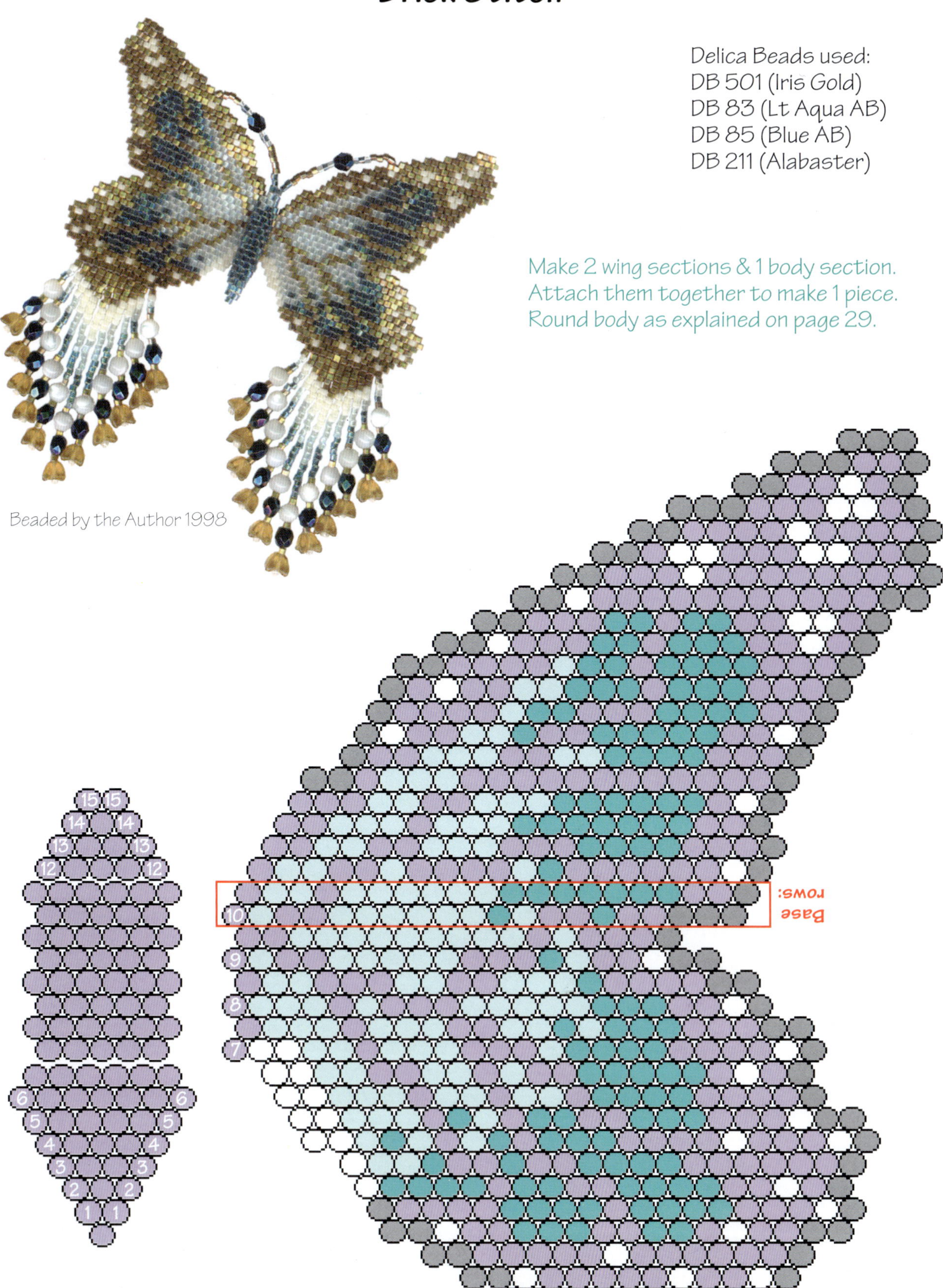

Beaded by the Author 1998

Delica Beads used:
DB 501 (Iris Gold)
DB 83 (Lt Aqua AB)
DB 85 (Blue AB)
DB 211 (Alabaster)

Make 2 wing sections & 1 body section.
Attach them together to make 1 piece.
Round body as explained on page 29.

Butterfly, Large Painted
Brick Stitch

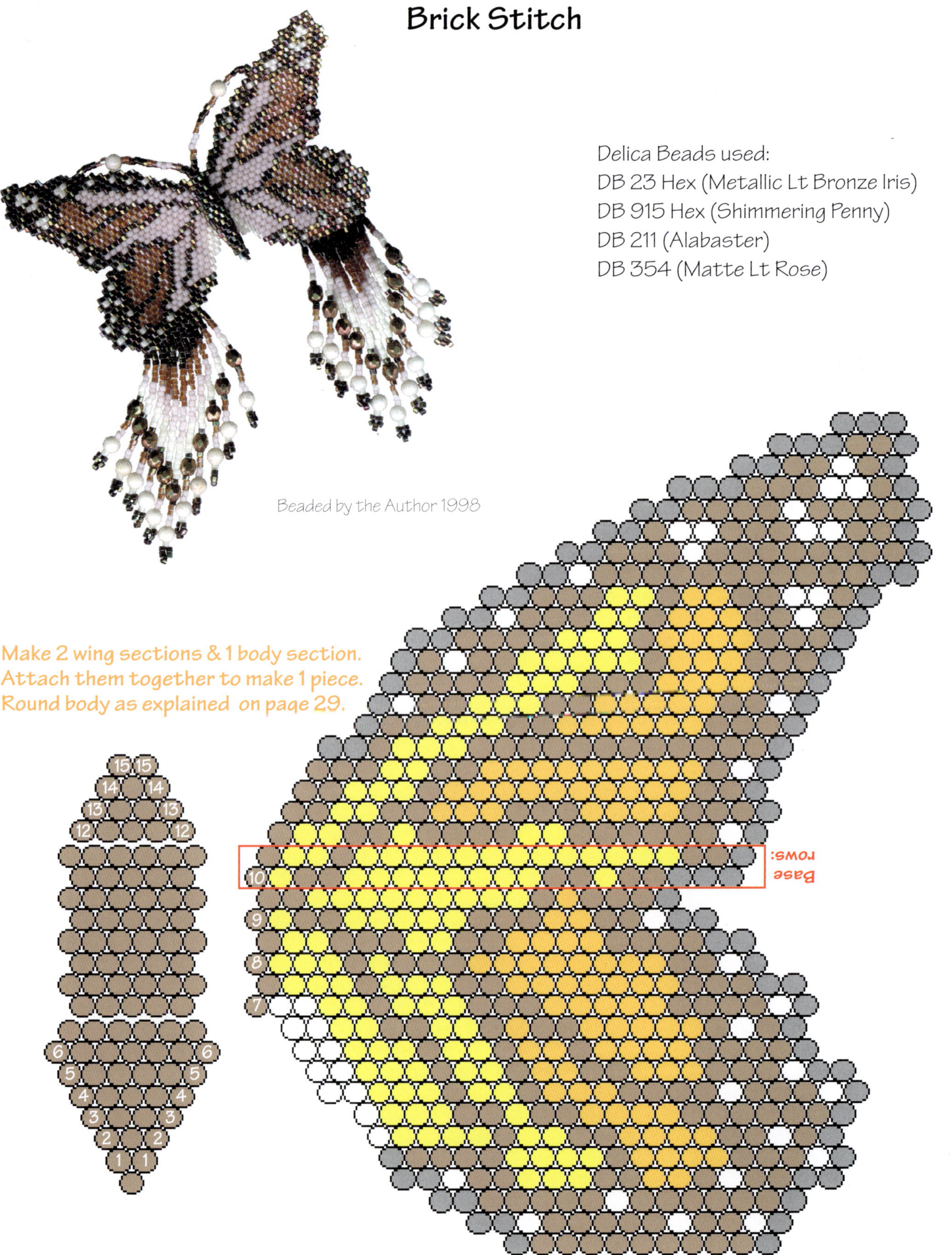

Delica Beads used:
DB 23 Hex (Metallic Lt Bronze Iris)
DB 915 Hex (Shimmering Penny)
DB 211 (Alabaster)
DB 354 (Matte Lt Rose)

Make 2 wing sections & 1 body section.
Attach them together to make 1 piece.
Round body as explained on page 29.

Beaded by the Author 1998

V-Branch Fringed Necklace

Brick Stitch & Branch Fringe
Using: Two (2) Colors of size 11 seed beads and 1 Cabochon (Apprimately 18 x 13mm)

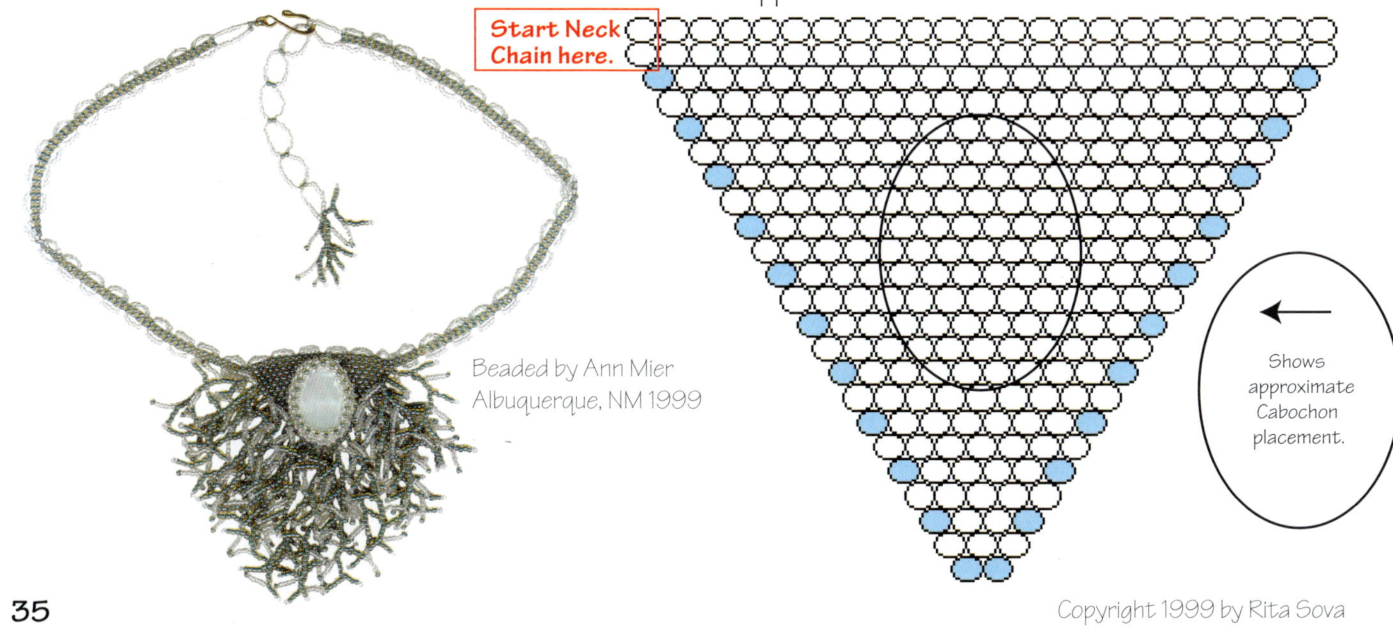

Basic Instructions

1. Create the above V-background. I used size 11 seed beads with a 23 bead base row.
   See page 56 for the One Bead Base Row Technique, replace 1 bead with 2 in each step.
   Use the Brick Stitch to complete the V-background shown above.
   Optional: Brick Stitch a design in your V-background or embellish it with flowers & charms.

2. Attach the cabochon to the V-background, remember positioning is important. I put a tiny
   bit of glue to hold the cabochon in place while I am using a peyote stitch to attach
   beads to the V-background then up around the cabochon. (A beaded Bezel) The beaded
   Bezel is what is really holding the cabochon in place not the glue.

3. Add Branch fringe to the Blue colored beads shown below.

Approximate Cabochon size: 18 x 13 mm.

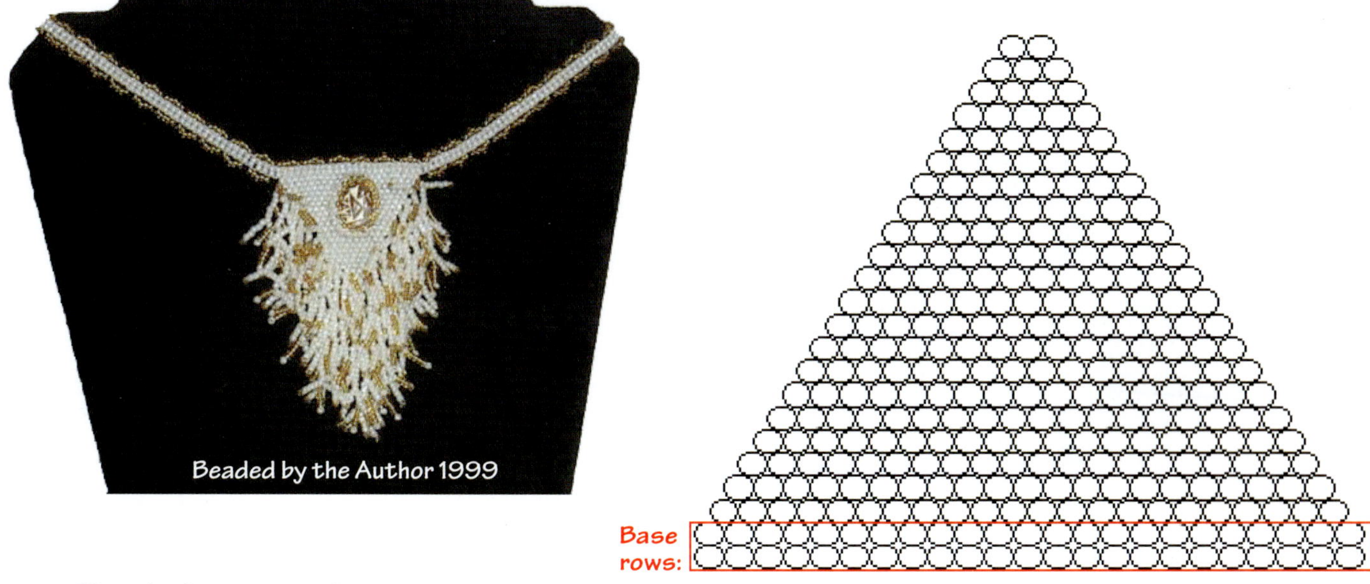

V-Branch Fringed Necklace
Branch Fringe basic instructions
Start fringe from one of the bottom 2 beads of background V:

FRINGE # 1

MAIN BRANCH: Pick up 28 Cream beads & 1 Blue bead.

1st BRANCH: Insert needle up through beads 28, 27, 26, 25, (the last 4 Cream beads).
The Blue bead is the turn around bead, it keeps the 28 beads from falling off.

BRANCH 2: Pick up 5 Blue & 1 Cream bead. Insert needle back through the 5 Blue beads & 3 beads on the original branch.

Repeat up the main branch, alternating colors as shown.

When you reach the top of each main branch, you will have to decide whether or not to add an extra branch to the main branch. This makes a fuller look at the top near cabochon. This would mean only going through 1 or 2 beads on the main branch before adding more branches.

To finish attaching the 1st main branch fringe to the V-background: Insert needle up through the opposite bead your thread started at. (of the 2 bottom blue beads)

Reposition needle to come down out of the next bead you want to add fringe too. (See page 35.)

FRINGE #2-35:
Repeat above: Except decrease 1 bead in each main branch for each fringe as you work up one side. Then reverse to match both sides of V. Insert needle back up through the same bead of the V-background as you originally started with for the rest of your fringe.

NECK CHAIN:
1.) You will use the one bead base row technique shown on page 56. Replace 1 bead with 2 in each step.
   Add 2 beads at a time next to the 2 top rows of the V-background.
2.) Add 4 sets of 2 Cream beads each.
3.) Add edging: pick up 5 Blue beads. Insert needle through the first 2 bead set added in step 2.
   These 5 beads will form an edge on the top/bottom of the chain.
   Pick up 5 Blue beads. Insert needle through the last 2 bead set added in step 2 to form the edge on the opposite side of the chain.
4.) Continue on: repeat steps 2-4 until desired length. Add clasp and you are done.

Goose Pin
Square Stitch

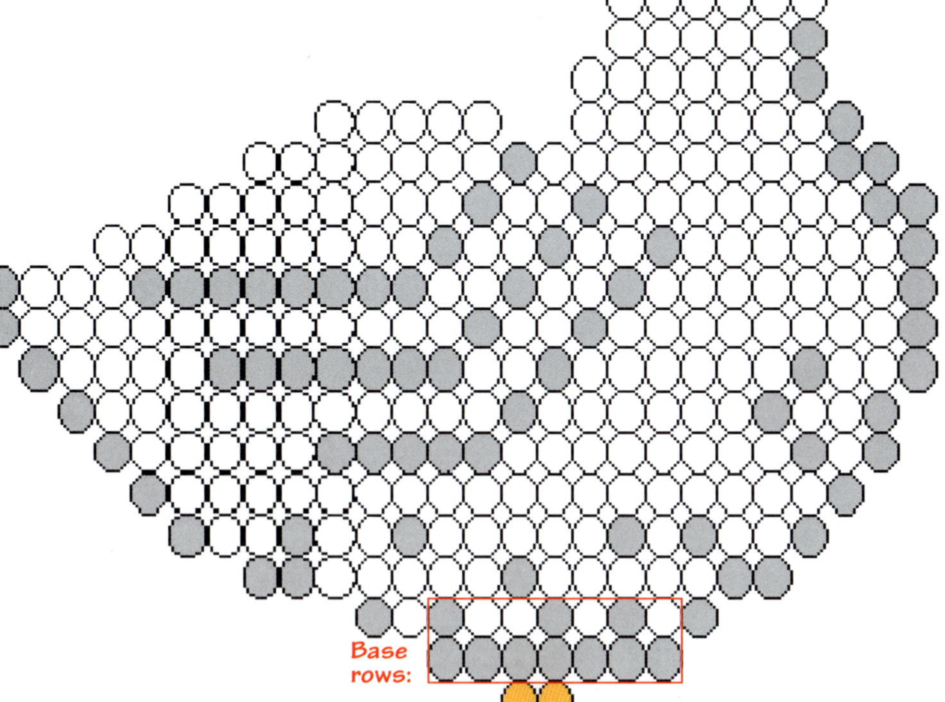

Delica Beads used:
DB 201 (White Pearl)
DB 252 (Ceylon Lt Gray)
DB 681 (S/L Squash)
DB 10 (Black)

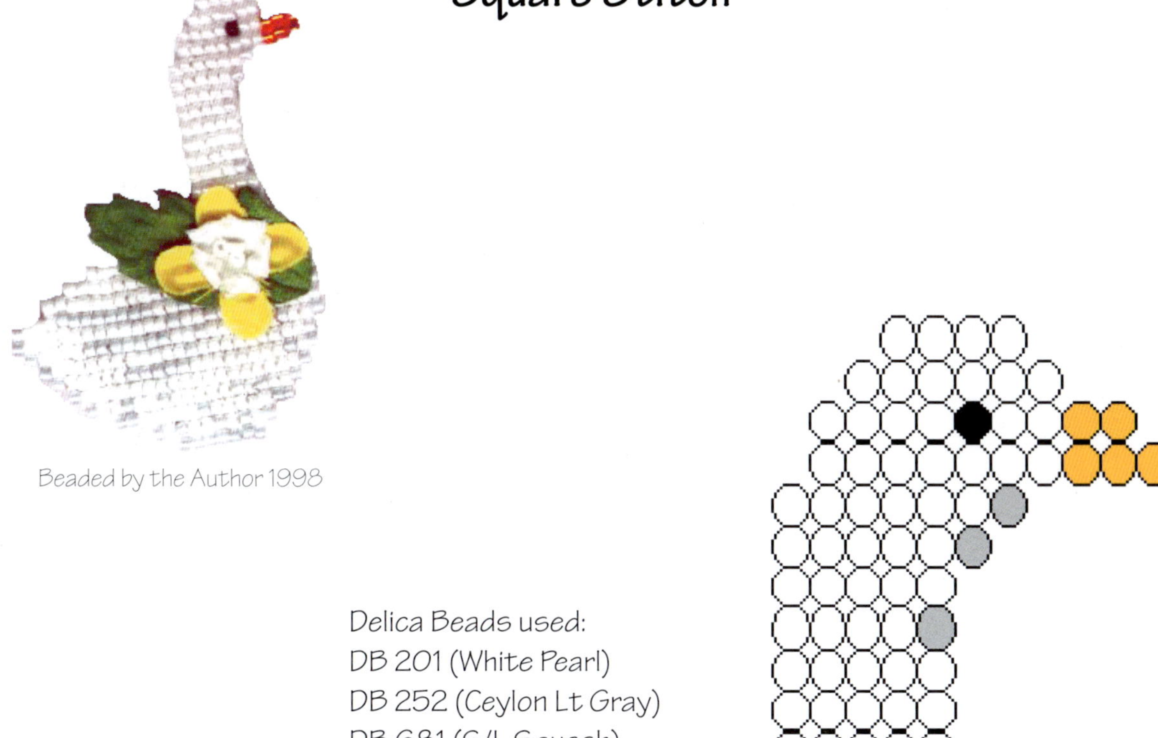

Panda Pin
Panda: Square Stitch
Wing: Brick Stitch

Beaded by the Author 1998

PANDA
Delica Beads used:
DB 202 (White Pearl AB)
DB 10 (Black)

PANDA
Delica Beads used:
DB 201 (White Pearl)
DB 10 (Black)

WINGS
Delica Beads used:
DB 27 (Met. Teal Iris)
DB 22L (Met. Lt. Bronze)

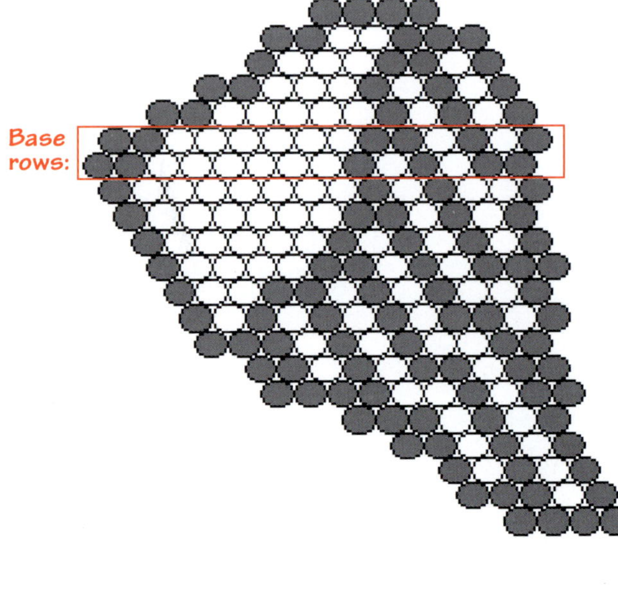

Penguin Pin
Square Stitch

Beaded by the Author 1998

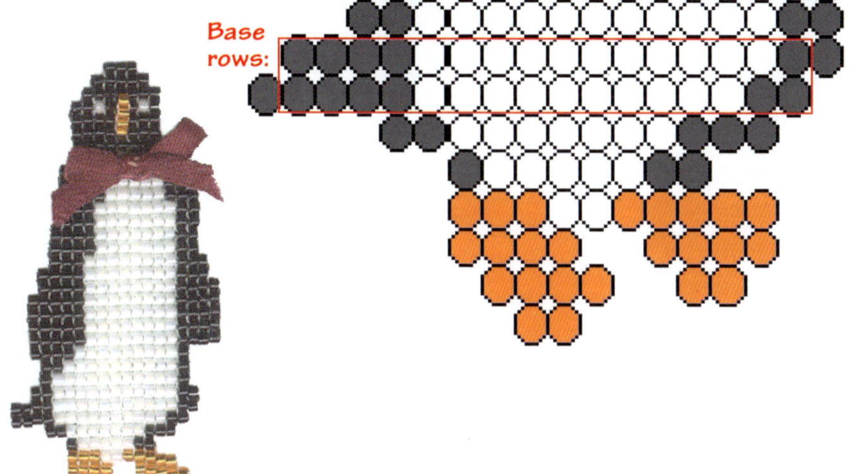

For a 3-D effect:
Add 2 beads sticking
straight out for the bill.
Add a ribbon bow tie!

Delica Beads used:
DB 201 (White Pearl)
DB 681 (S/L Squash)
DB 10 (Black)

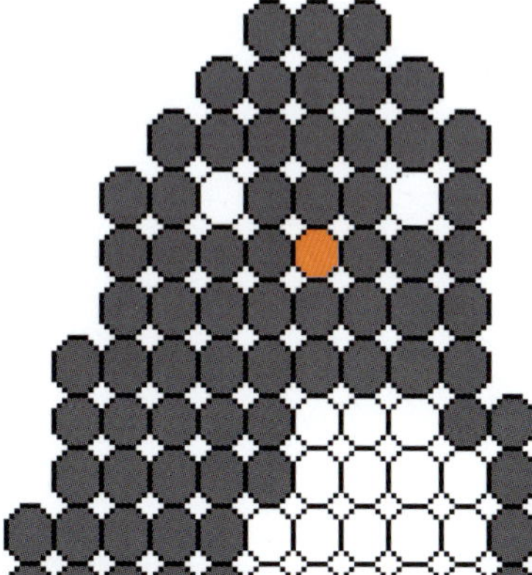

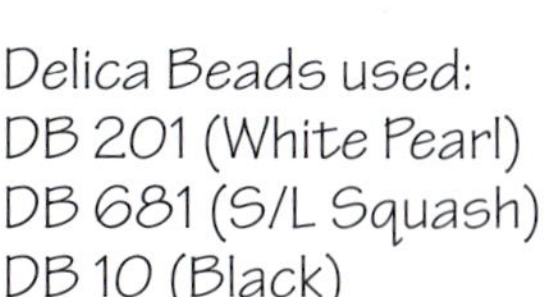

St. Therese Picture
Square Stitch

Beaded by the Author 1999

Delica Beads used:
DB 42 (S/L Gold-Edge)
DB 10 (Black-Lettering & Habit)
DB 697 (Semi Matte S/L Gray-Habit Shading)
DB 731 (Opaque Gray-Habit Shading)
DB 208 (Opaque Tan-Face/Hand)
DB 69 (Lnd Beige AB-Face/Hand Shading)
DB 741 (Matte Trsp Crystal-Fingernails)
DB 915 (Lnd Shimmering Penny-Lips)
DB 321 (Matte Metallic Silver-Jesus Background)
DB 78 (Lnd Aqua Mist-Background)
DB 878 (Matte Aqua-Background)
DB 852 (Matte Tan-Background)
DB 853 (Matte Dk Tan-Background)
DB 857 (Matte Trsp Lt Amethyst AB-Background)
DB 356 (Matte Medium Amethyst-Background)
DB 62 (Lnd Strawberry Ice AB-Flower)
DB 723 (Opaque Red-Flower)
DB 27 (Metallic Teal Iris-Leaves)
DB 178 (Trsp Cobalt AB-Eyes)
DB 200 (Opaque Chalk White-Collar)
DB 252 (Ceylon Gray-Collar Shading)
DB 38 (Dk White Gold 22 Kt-Necklace)
DB 211 (Alabaster-Gown)
DB 203 (Ceylon Lt. Yellow-Gown)
DB 907 (Lnd Crystal/Shimmering Sand-Gown)

This is no small project, please be warned. It took me about 2-1/2 months to complete the beading of St. Therese. I was not working on it full time. This pattern is 139 rows wide by 177 rows long. The completed picture using Delica Beads measures 8"wide by 12"long.

St. Therese Picture Pattern

Base rows (139 wide):

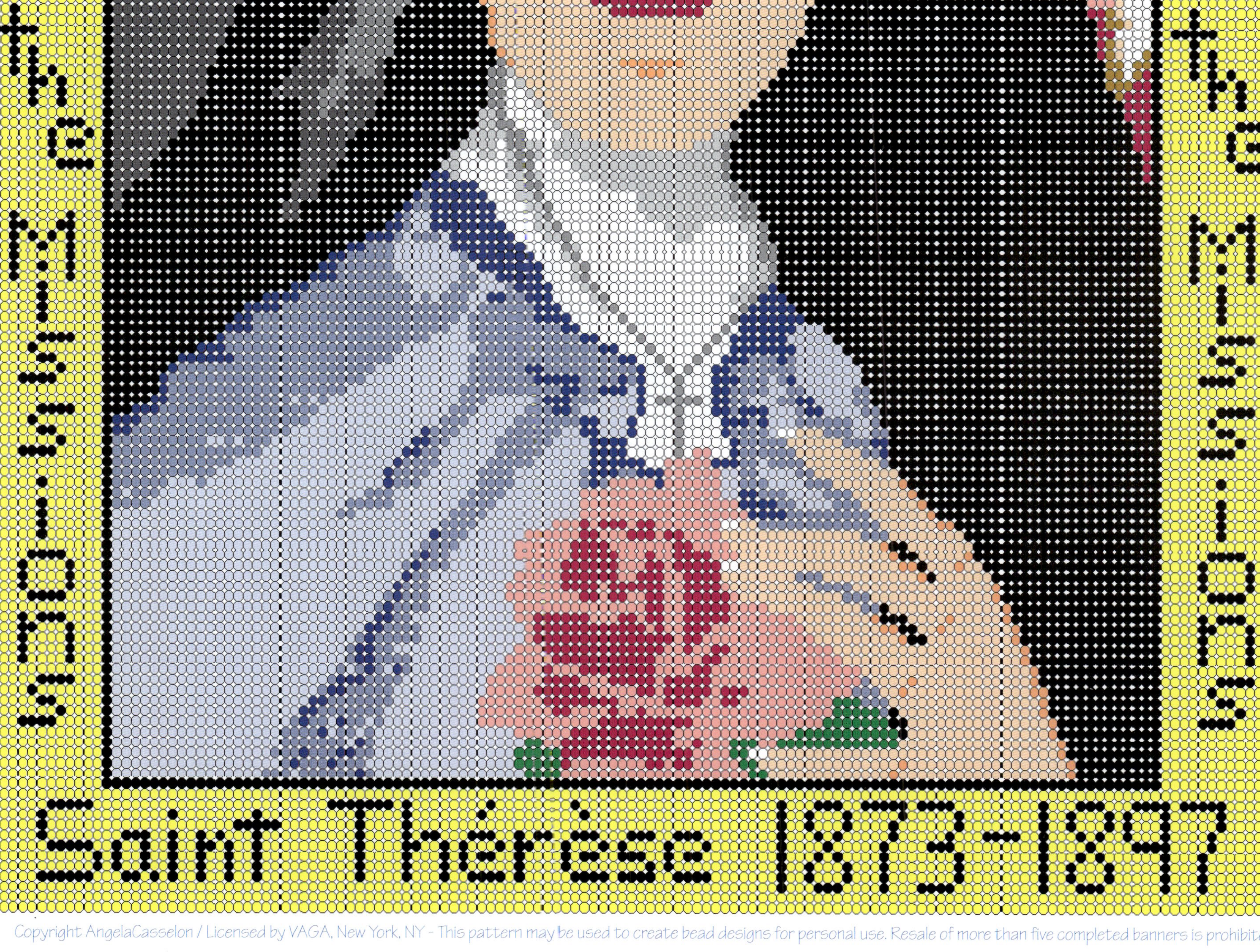
the Missions
the Missions
Saint Thérèse 1873-1897

Heart Choker
Square Stitch

No Metal Clasp!
Using 3 colors of size 11 Seed Beads

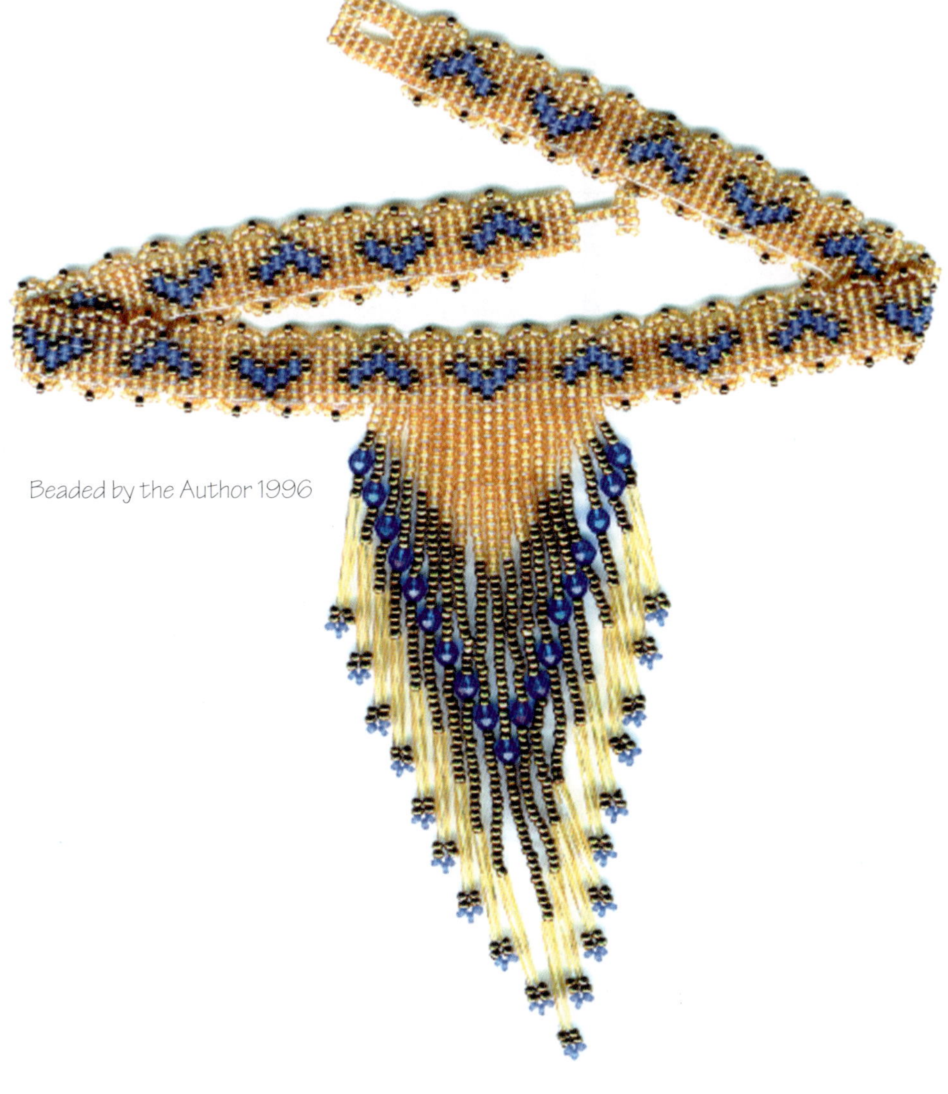

Take your neck measurement and add 1/2". This is your desired length.
Repeat the Heart pattern as many times as needed to reach your desired length.
Fringe and edging are always your option. Short, Long or None....

Celtic Bracelet
Square Stitch

Base rows:

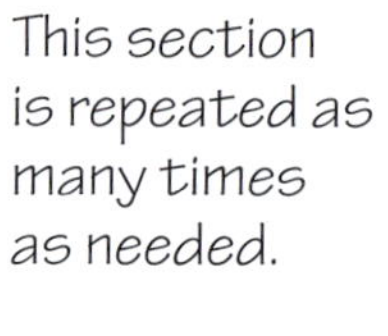

This section is repeated as many times as needed.

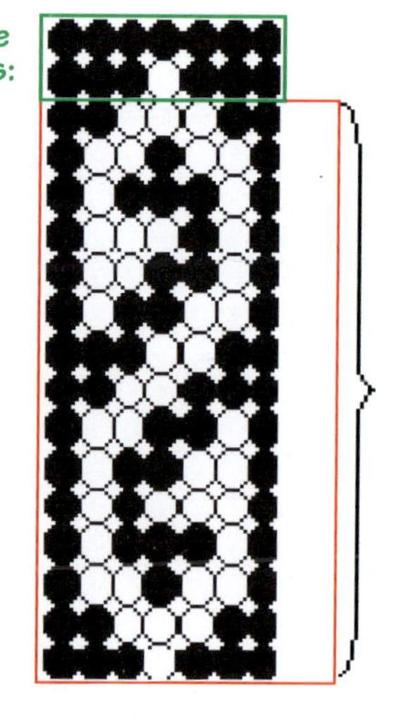

Delica Beads used:
DB 10 (Black)
DB 906 (Lnd Lavender)

Eagle Belt Buckle
Square Stitch

Size 11 Japanese Seed Beads
& 3-1/4" x 2" belt buckle blank.

Beaded by Jo Ann Roybal
Santa Fe New Mexico 1999

Thanks Jo, designed by your request. "A Guy Thing"

46 wide x 25 high

Bichon Pin
Square Stitch

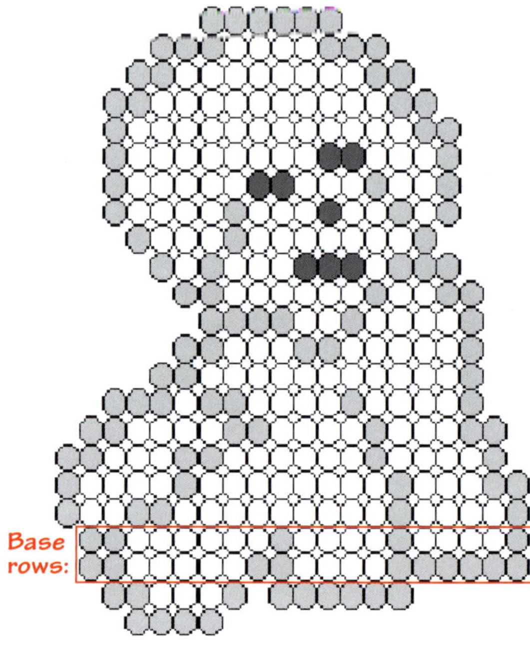

Delica Beads used:
DB 201 (White Pearl)
DB 322 (Matte Metallic Gold)
DB 105 (Dk Red Luster)
DB 27 (Metallic Teal Iris)

Beaded by the Author 1998

With Red Chili

Without Red Chili

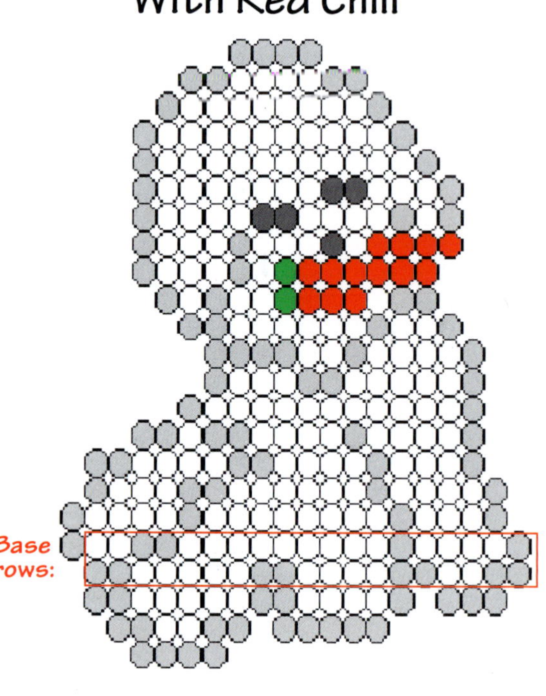

Christmas Ornament the Fish Net
Net Weave Technique
Using size 11 seed beads & a 35mm Christmas Ornament

Beaded by the Author 1999

Any 2 colors of size 11 seed beads will work nicely. I used the larger size 11 seed beads.

Ornaments (50mm) with small top caps: A bead count of 28 is used for row 1. Omit beads 2, 10, 18 & 26 of row 1.

○○ White Beads   ◐◐ Gold Beads

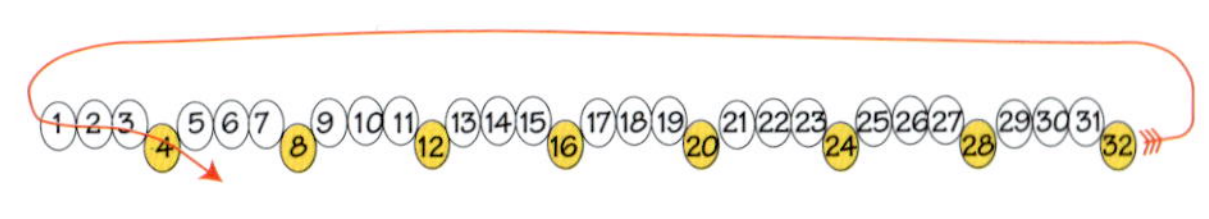

Row 1 Set=3-1: Pick up 32 beads (8 sets … as shown above).
Insert needle through all beads about 2 times to secure your top circle. Make sure this circle fits over the top of the ornament. Thread should exit gold bead number 4 shown above. You are ready for row 2.

Row 2 set = 4-1-4: Pick up 4-1-4. Insert needle through bead 8 of row one. Repeat pick up 4-1-4. Insert needle through bead 12 of row one. Repeat to the end of the row as shown below.

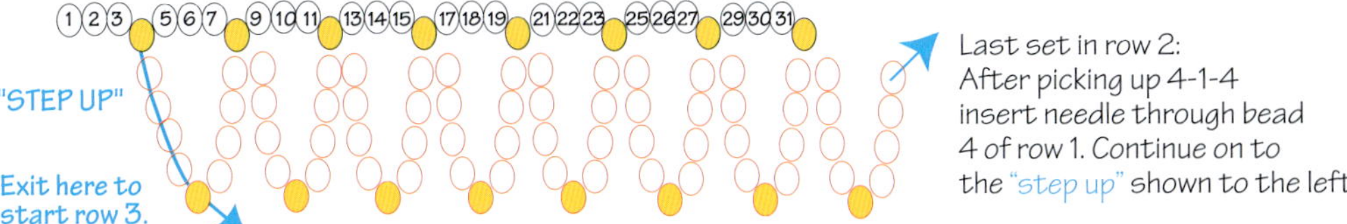

"STEP UP"

Exit here to start row 3.

Last set in row 2: After picking up 4-1-4 insert needle through bead 4 of row 1. Continue on to the "step up" shown to the left.

Step Up: After adding the last bead set of a particular row you will insert needle through the first few beads (listed below) to create your "Step up" to the next row.

Keep work snug for a nice fit. For the next rows follow the bead count below. The Net Weave can be used on all kinds of objects: All sizes of ornaments, beads, bottles, crystals, etc…

Bead Count		"Step up" Beads
Rows 3 & 4:	5 Gold, 1 White, 5 Gold	5 Gold, 1 White
Rows 5 & 6:	6 White, 1 Gold, 6 White	6 White, 1 Gold
Row 7:	6 Gold, 1 White, 6 Gold	6 Gold, 1 White
Row 8:	5 Gold, 1 White, 5 Gold	5 Gold, 1 White
Row 9:	5 White, 1 Gold, 5 White	5 White, 1 Gold
Row 10:	4 White, 1 Gold, 4 White	4 White, 1 Gold
Rows 11 & 12:	4 Gold, 1 White, 4 Gold	4 Gold, 1 White
Row 13:	1 White	

Weave threads to secure. Fringe is optional.

When you change bead size (11) or ornament size (50mm), you must adjust the pattern to compensate.

Christmas Ornament the Fish Net
Net Weave Technique
Using size 11 seed beads, #3 Bugle beads & 50mm Christmas Ornament

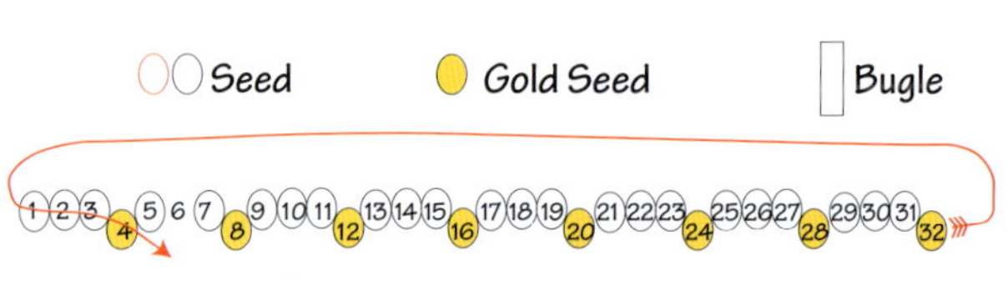

Beaded by the Author 1999

Any 2 colors of size 11 seed beads will work nicely. I used the larger size 11 seed beads. Size #3 Bugle beads are a must. I doubled my thread on this ornament because bugle beads often have sharp edges.

Ornaments (50mm) with small top caps: A bead count of 28 is used for row 1. Omit beads 2, 10, 18 & 26 of row 1.

◯◯ Seed   🟡 Gold Seed   ▯ Bugle

Row 1 Set=3-1: Pick up 32 beads (8 sets ... as shown above). Insert needle through all beads about 2 times to secure your top circle. Make sure this circle fits over the top of the ornament. Thread should exit gold bead number 4 shown above. You are ready for row 2.

Row 2 set = 1-Seed, 1-Bugle, 3-Seed, 1-Bugle, 1-Seed: Pick up all 7 beads. Insert needle through bead 8 of row one. Repeat: pick up 7 bead, insert needle through bead 12 of row one. Repeat to the end of the row.

"STEP UP"

Exit here to start row 3.

Last set in row 2: After picking up the last set insert needle through bead 4 of row 1. Continue on to the "step up" shown to the left.

Step Up: After adding the last bead set of a particular row you will insert needle through the first few beads (listed below) to create your "Step up" to the next row.

Keep work snug for a nice fit. For the next rows follow the bead count below. The Net Weave can be used on all kinds of objects: All sizes of ornaments, beads, bottles, crystals, etc...

<table>
<tr><td colspan="2">Bead Count</td></tr>
<tr><td>Rows 3 & 4 & 5:</td><td>1-Seed. 1-Bugle, 1-Seed, 1-Bugle, 3-Seed, 1-Bugle, 1-Seed, 1-Bugle, 1-Seed</td></tr>
<tr><td>"Step up" Beads:</td><td>1-Seed. 1-Bugle, 1-Seed, 1-Bugle, 2-Seed</td></tr>
<tr><td>Row 6:</td><td>1 Gold Seed</td></tr>
<tr><td colspan="2" align="center">Weave threads to secure. Fringe is optional.</td></tr>
</table>

When you change bead size (11) or ornament size (50mm), you must adjust the pattern to compensate.

Christmas Ornaments
Net Weave Technique
For 50mm Christmas Ornament

Please refer to pages 47 & 48 for the Net Weave Technique used for these 2 ornaments

Beaded by the Author 1999

The Fancy Bugle Fish Net

Any 2 colors of size 11 seed beads will work nicely. I used thelarger size 11 seed beads. Size #3 Bugle beads & 4mm Crystals are a must. I doubled my thread on this ornament because bugle beads often have sharp edges.

○ White Seed   ● Gold Seed   ▮ Gold Bugle   ◇ Crystal 4mm

Row 1:	32 bead top circle as in previous patterns. (3-White, 1-Gold Seed)
Row 2:	2-White, 1-Bugle, 2-White, 1-4mm, 2-White, 1-Bugle, 2-White
Rows 3, 4 & 5:	Repeat row 2.
Row 6:	2-White, 1-Bugle, 3-White, 1-Bugle, 2-White
Row 7:	1-Gold Seed

Ornaments (50mm) with small top caps:
A bead count of 28 is used for row 1.
Omit beads 2, 10, 18 & 26 of row 1.

The Diamond V Net

Any 2 colors of size 11 seed beads will work nicely. I used the larger size 11 seed beads. Size #5 Bugle beads & 4mm Crystals are a must. I doubled my thread on this ornament because bugle beads often have sharp edges.

Beaded by the Author 1999

● Blue Seed   ○ White Seed   ▯ Crystal Bugle   ◇ Crystal 4mm

Row 1:	32 bead top circle as in previous patterns. (3-Blue Seed, 1-White Seed)
Row 2:	5-Blue, 1-Bugle, 5-Blue, 1-White Seed, 5-Blue, 1-Bugle, 5-Blue
Row 3:	5-Blue, 1-4mm, 5-Blue
Row 4:	5-Blue, 1-White Seed, 5-Blue
Row 5:	Repeat row 2.
Row 6:	3-Blue

Net Weave Choker

Net Weave Technique
2 Colors of size 11 Seed Beads

Row 1: Create a single strand of beads: pattern 1-5-1-5-1. Repeat until desired length. 1-5 is a set, you will use the center 20 sets to add your net weave from. Don't forget your clasp. Have thread exiting bead marked "start here", (needle should aim toward center), you are now ready for row 2.

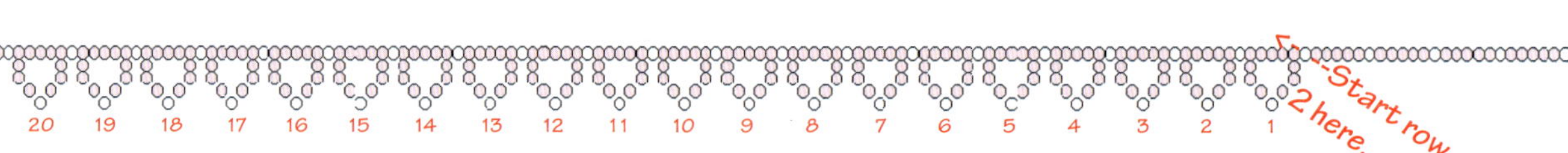

Row 2 set = 3-1-3, Add 20 sets as shown.

After picking up 1st set, insert needle into next clear bead to the left on the main chain. Repeat to the end.
Turn Around/Step Down: insert needle back through the last 3-1 beads added.

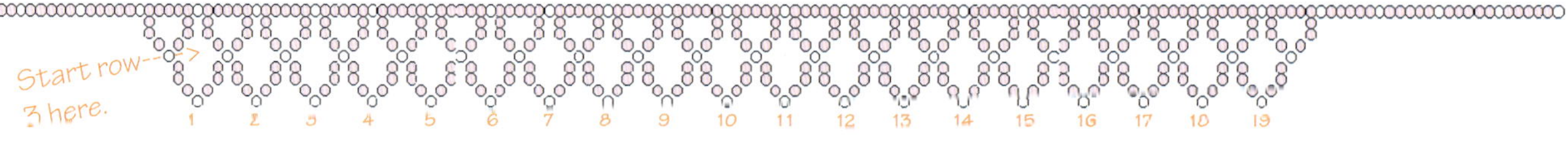

Row 3 set = 3-1-3, Add 19 sets as shown.

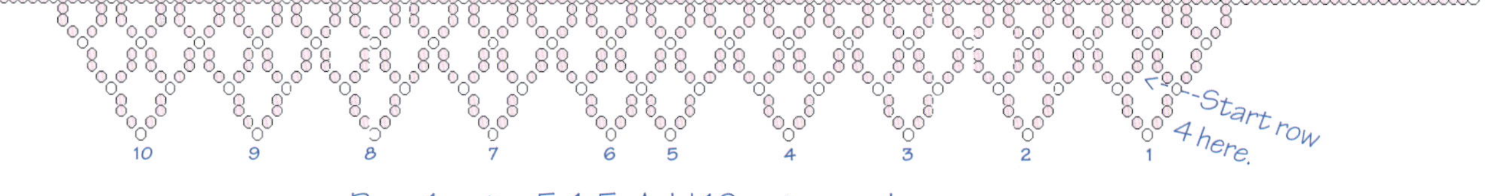

Row 4 set = 5-1-5, Add 10 sets as shown.

Row 5 set = 5-1-5, Add 1 set as shown. You may also add your fringe/dangles now.

Feather Twist Necklace

Round Peyote & Fringe
I used 3 colors of size 11 Japanese Seed Beads

Beaded by the Author 1998

First you will create a peyote chain to your desired length. My sample was 17" long before the fringe was added. In the center of this chain you will use 32 beads to attach the fringe to. Please see the 32 bead example on the following page. I made an 8 bead circle, but others have done 9 & 7 bead peyote chains and it still works. The fringe uses quite a few beads and adds a lot of weight to the chain. If your stitching is loose your chain will stretch even further. When sizing allow 1-2" in chain for stretch.

Feather Twist Necklace
Fringe Bead Count & Number of Twists

Insert needle up through the 5th purple bead from the tan (marked 1 below), of the peyote chain.
Pick up beads for fringe 1 as listed in columns below until the turn around column.
Add turn around beads. Insert needle up through the last purple bead added, snug. Fringe #1 will not twist.
Add remainder of fringe beads. Insert needle up though next bead over (2) in the peyote chain; always insert the needle the same direction. This will make a nicer finished product. Try it, you will be amazed.

Twist(s) - Always twist in the same direction, in this case up, always up. Twists will be done around the previous fringe added. Insert needle up-from back to front under the 1st strand of fringe nearest to the fringe you are adding. Repeat for the number of twists shown and secure into next bead in peyote chain.

Sample: 32 beads for center of necklace for fringe placement.

Fringe Number	Cream Beads	Tan Beads	Purple Beads	Turn Around	Twist Up	Purple Beads	Tan Beads	Cream Beads
1 - 31			25	2T-3C-2T	0	24		
2 - 30			28	Same	2	27		
3 - 29			31	Same	2	30		
4 - 28			34	Same	2	33		
5 - 27		5	32	Same	2	31	5	
6 - 26		5	35	Same	2	34	5	
7 - 25	3	5	35	Same	2	34	5	3
8 - 24	8	5	33	Same	2	32	5	8
9 - 23	11	5	33	Same	2	32	5	11
10 - 22	16	5	32	Same	3	31	5	16
11 - 21	19	5	32	Same	3	31	5	19
12 - 20	22	5	32	Same	3	31	5	22
13 - 19	28	5	28	Same	3	27	5	28
14 - 18	31	5	28	Same	3	27	5	31
15 - 17	34	5	28	Same	3	27	5	34
16	37	5	28	Same	3	27	5	37

31 Fringe will use 32 beads from peyote chain.

Butterfly Appliqué - Hair Ornament

Backstitch or Applique Technique
Use whatever beads you prefer.

Beaded by Jo Ann Roybal
Santa Fe, NM 1999

Use this pattern as a guide. Follow whichever lines you prefer.

1. Trace or copy applique' to your desired backing material.

2. Trim applique to desire shape. I like to bead the outside edge first. I get very very close to the edge of the backing material so the beads completely cover the edge and the backing does not show.

3. Fill in the pattern using the backstitch technique.

4. After filling in the pattern above, finish as desired. This can be used as a Hair Ornament as shown, or a patch for clothing-purse-whatever. Make a collection and hang them on the wall!

Have fun, so many colors & beads to choose from.

Basic Backstitch: Tie a knot in your thread (thread is not doubled), Insert needle from back to front through your desired backing material. (I used Stiff-Stuff.) Pick up 3 beads. Slide them all the way to the end of the thread. Insert needle from front to back at the end of the third bead added. Insert needle from back to front between beads 1 & 2, snug. Insert needle through beads 2 & 3. Pick up 3 beads and repeat. You can use 3 or more beads. I like to backstitch at least half of the beads added at one time.

X's & O's Necklace

This is a basic chain design and has many possibilities.
Play, have fun, create your own masterpiece.

○ Cream seed   ● Brown Seed   ⬡ 3 or 4mm

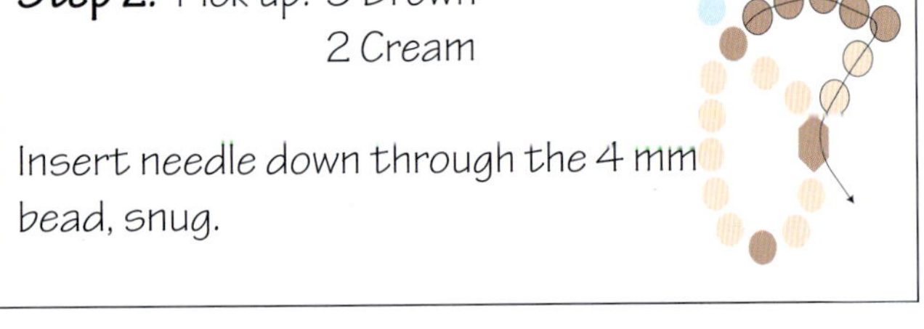

Using size 11's
Bead by the Author 1999

Using size 15's
Bead by the Author 1999

**First you will create the X's to
your desired length, then add the O's.**

X's: Start with approximately 3 yards of thread. You may add a stop bead at the end to keep beads from falling off. Leave a tail to to work in later or use for the O's section of this chain. Thread is not doubled.

Step 1: Pick up: 1 Brown
5 Cream
1 Brown
2 Cream
1-4 mm Brown
2 Cream

Insert needle up through 1st Brown bead added.
Both threads are coming out of the same bead.

Step 2: Pick up: 5 Brown
2 Cream

Insert needle down through the 4 mm bead, snug.

Step 3:
Pick up: 2 Cream
1 Brown
2 Cream
1-4 mm Brown
2 Cream

Insert needle up through the last Brown bead added in step 2, snug.

Repeat steps 2 & 3 until desired length is reached.

End with step 3 and make both beginning & end match.

O's:

This is the fringe section: Start at one end of the chain. Thread should exit brown bead as shown. ●

Fringe 1: Pick up 9 brown beads.
Insert needle through bead shown. ●

Fringe 2: Pick up 9 brown beads.
Insert needle through the next brown bead shown. ●

Fringe 3: Pick up 10 brown beads.
Insert needle through the next brown bead shown. ●

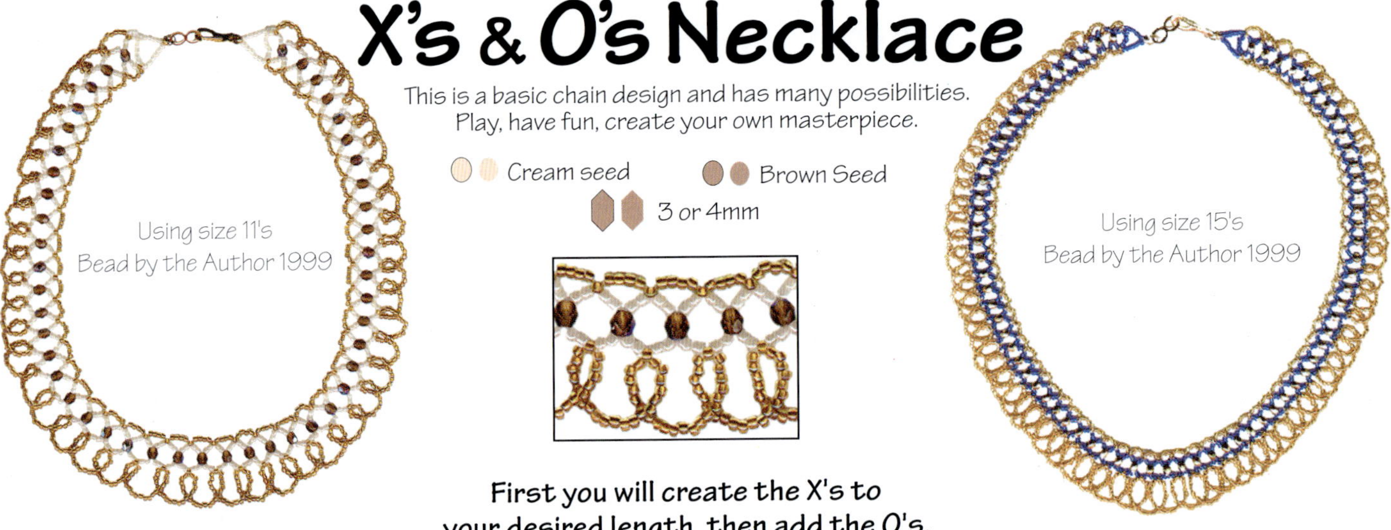

Next Fringe: repeat the above - For the size of chains shown. I used the above method of increasing by 1 bead on all odd numbered fringe until I reached the center. I then reversed the count to make both sides match. Don't forget your clasp. You made it.

General Rules:

1. Read all material and check supplies before beginning.
2. I usually use Nymo thread, size B and a size 10 beading needle.
3. You will NOT tie knots unless specifically told to. To end or start new thread you will weave: in, out, back & forth, beads until thread is secure. Thread should not be showing between or over beads. Then thread may be cut.
4. I usually start with 2-1/2 to 3 yards of thread. Any more than that and I have too many knotting problems. Thread is not doubled.
5. Put your pattern into a clear protective sheet and use an erasable marker to keep track of where you are, you can reuse patterns again & again.
6. The use of wax or thread conditioners is optional: these products make your thread easier to handle (among other things). Anything thread can find to wrap around, including itself, it will!
7. Patterns are read in a zigzag fashion from row to row. Base row(s)=left to right, next row=right to left, next row=left to right, etc... Sometimes you will need to turn the pattern upside down in order to see your beginning triangle. Just leave it upside down and bead.
8. These instructions are written from a right hander's point of view. I hold the beads between my left thumb and forefinger and the needle in my right hand. I always work from left to right. (Reading the pattern is still done in the zigzag fashion.)

> **UP:** the needlepoint is pointing up (toward the sky or your face).
> **DOWN:** the needlepoint is pointed down (toward the floor or your lap).

Circle Stitch:

Example 1: You have 2 beads you want to join together. 1 bead is attached to bead work already. Thread is coming out of the top of that bead: Pick up a bead. Insert needle up through the bead the thread is coming out of.

Ending or Adding Threads: Some beads are stitched together. Thread is coming out of the top of a bead. Insert needle down one bead on the left (or right) side of the bead your thread is coming out of. Insert needle up through the same bead you started with.

Basic Brick Stitch Instructions

2 Bead Base Row Technique

NOT let go of the 3 bead triangle made in step 1 while adding the 2 beads in steps 2 & 3. Only snug beads after step 3 is completed. To snug the beads, pull the thread up and slightly to the left.

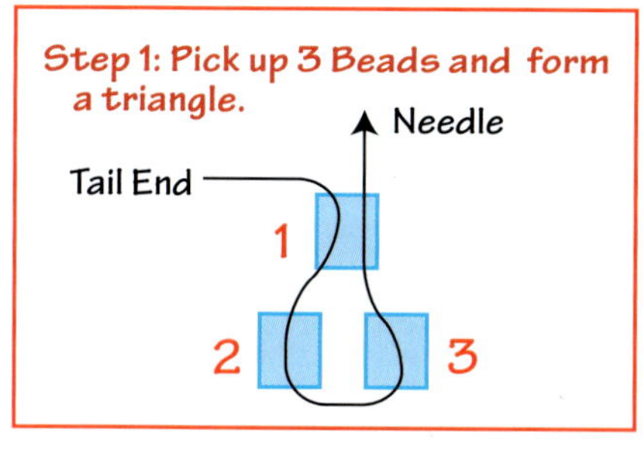

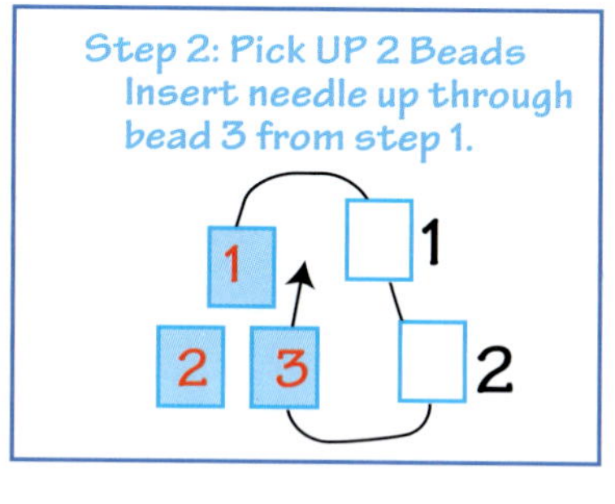

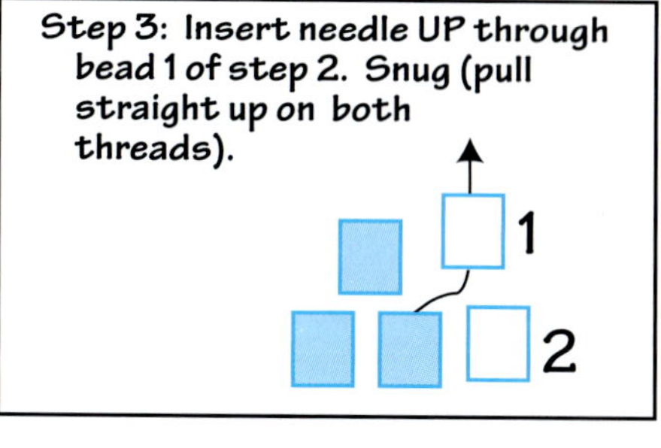

STEP 1: Read pattern left to right for base row(s). Pick up 3 beads (numbered above). Insert needle into bead 1 and form a triangle as shown. Hold this triangle securely. If you let go before step 3 is completed you will have to start over.

STEP 2: Pick up 2 new beads (numbered above-the top bead first). Insert needle UP bead 3 of triangle, make sure your needle is in front of the thread coming out of bead 1 of the triangle (needle closer to you). Gently pull excess thread until the 2 new beads are close to the triangle. The first bead added will be on top as shown above.

STEP 3: Insert needle UP the bead that ended up on top (bead 1 in step 2). Make sure the needle is behind the thread coming out bead 2 of the triangle (thread should be closer to you now). SNUG, you can let go of the triangle beads NOW.

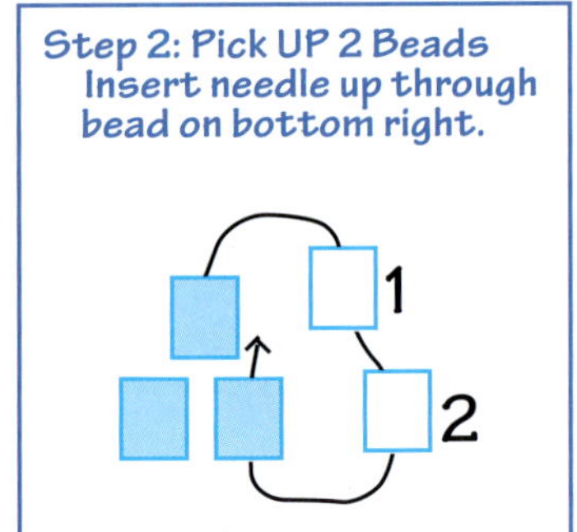

Repeat steps 2 & 3 to the end of the base rows.

One Bead Base Row Technique

1. Pick up the first 2 beads, let them go toward the end of your thread, leave a tail end that you can work in later.

2. Insert needle through bead 1, pull. Beads should sit side by side.

3. Insert needle down through bead 2. You are ready for bead 3.

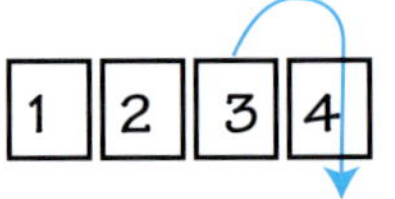

4. Pick up bead 3. Insert needle down bead 2, snug.

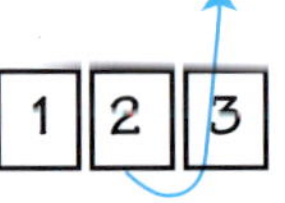

5. Insert needle up through bead 3. You are ready for bead 4.

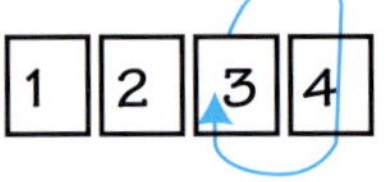

6. Pick up bead 4. Insert needle up bead 3, snug.

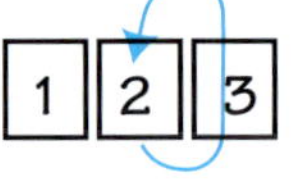

7. Insert needle down through bead 4. You are ready for bead 5.

Repeat to the end of your base row.

You can use 2 or 3 beads in place of 1 as in the Balloon Pins or Heart Earrings. This may also be used for Bugle bead base rows. It is probably the most common way to start a brick stitch design. The 2 bead base row technique is faster for some patterns.

Brick Stitch

STEP 1- Beginning of every row: You will always pick up 2 beads at the beginning of each row,

Step 1: Pick up 2 beads, insert needle under the loop of thread between beads 2 & 3 of the top row, snug.

Step 2: Insert needle up bead 2 of the two beads just added, snug.

Step 3: Circle Stitch beads 1 & 2 together. *Insert needle down through bead 1 of the two beads just added. Insert needle up bead 2 of the two beads just added.*
(* to * = a circle stitch)

Step 4: Single beads: The rest of the beads are added 1 at a time.
Pick up 1 bead. Insert needle under the next loop of thread, snug. Insert needle up through the bead you just added.
Repeat step 4 to the end of the row.

Increase - beginning of row:
Pick up 2 beads as usual. Insert needle under loop between beads 1 & 2 (instead of 2 & 3). Everything else is the same. If there is more than a 1 bead increase: use the increase method above, then use the circle stitch to add more from there.

Increase - end of row:
When you have run out of loops between beads, use the circle stitch to add more beads to this row.

Decrease - beginning of row:
You must reposition your thread to come out of another bead before starting this row.

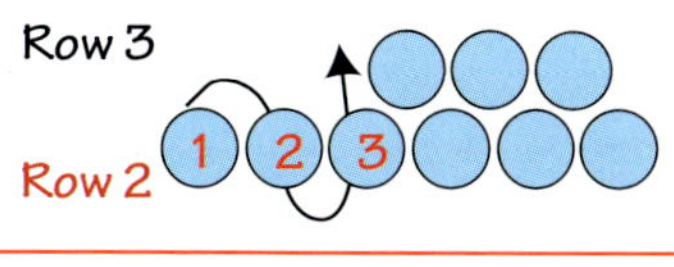

Example: Row 3 is missing 2 beads at the beginning of the row. You can insert needle down bead 2, snug. Insert needle up bead 3, snug. You are now ready to start row 3. Always pick up 2 beads at the beginning of each row.

Example 2:
When 1 bead is missing in row 3, you must reposition your thread to come out of bead 2 in row 2 before starting row 3.

Decrease - end of row:
You just stop and start the next row.

** There is more than one way to do some of these techniques, I say "try it my way, then do what feels right and looks good for you". Each project is different, so dare to explore.
Most of all have fun.

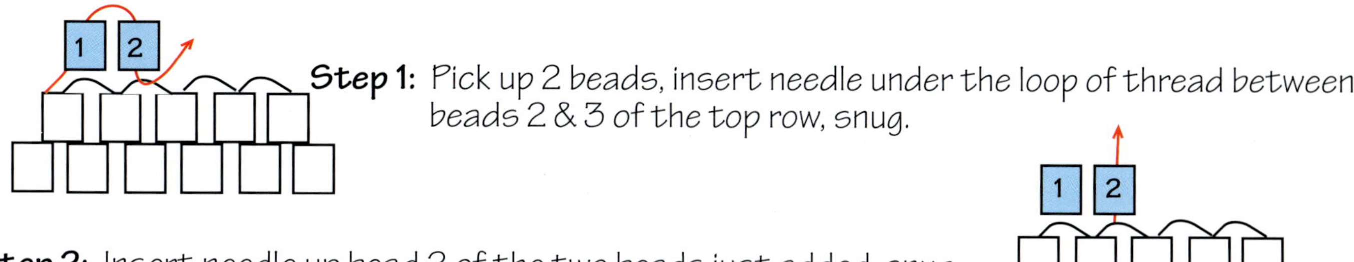

Flat Peyote Stitch (Even Count)

1. Pick up all beads for rows 1 and 2. I marked these with X's on my patterns. Leave a tail to weave in later. You may add a stop bead (keeps beads from falling of tail end until they become secure). Remove the "stop" bead when beads are secure.

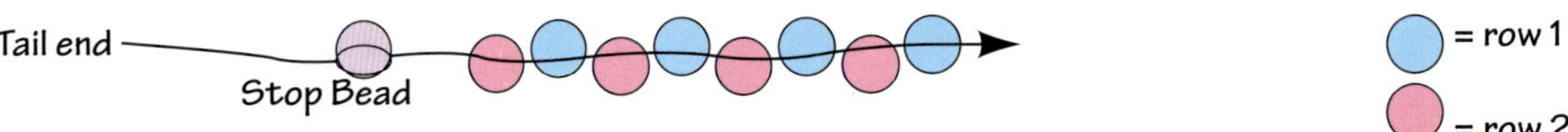

2. Row 3: Pick up one bead. Skip last bead in row 1. Insert needle through the last bead in row 2.

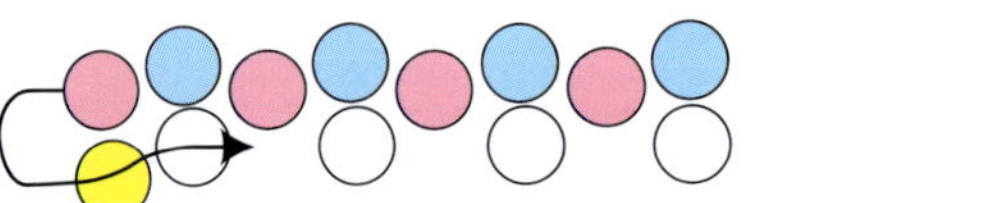

3. Repeat to end of row 3: Pick up one bead, skip a row 1 bead, insert needle through the next row 2 bead.

4. Row 4: As in row 3 you are filling in the holes. Repeat the above to finish.

Zipping the sides together:

1. Circle stitch the 2 end beads together.

2. Follow the path. Only going through the beads sticking out on either edge.

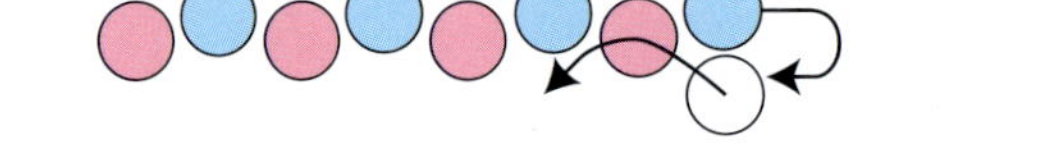

3. Circle stitch the other 2 end beads together to finish zipping up the sides.

Basic Instructions
for Tubular Peyote Stitch
(Even Count)

1. Pick up 8 beads for rows 1 and 2. Insert needle through bead 1 and form a circle.

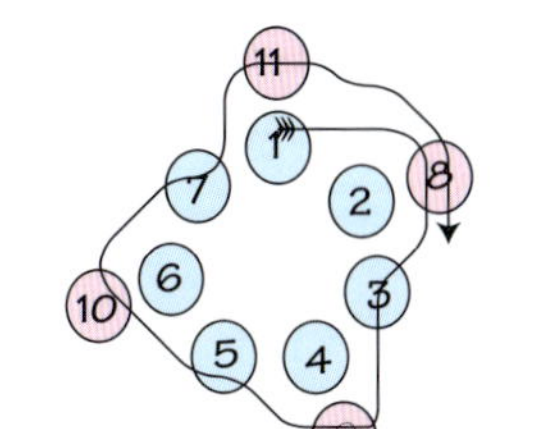

2. Pick up 1 bead (9). Insert needle through bead 3.
3. Pick up 1 bead (10). Insert needle through bead 5.
4. Pick up 1 bead (11). Insert needle through bead 7.
5. Pick up 1 bead (12). Insert needle through bead 1.

STEP UP:
Insert needle through bead 9 (first bead in row 3).

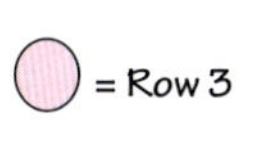
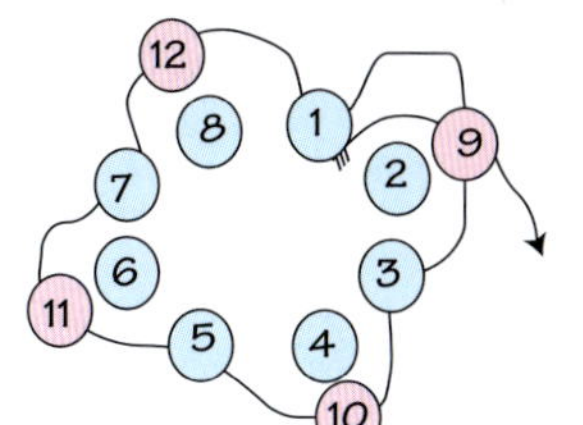

6. Pick up 1 bead (13). Insert needle through bead 10.
7. Pick up 1 bead (14). Insert needle through bead 11.
8. Pick up 1 bead (15). Insert needle through bead 12.
9. Pick up 1 bead (16). Insert needle through bead 9.

STEP UP:
Insert needle through bead 13.

Repeat until desired length is met.

Basic Instructions
for Tubular Peyote Stitch
(odd count)

There is no step up when using the odd Tubular Peyote Stitch.

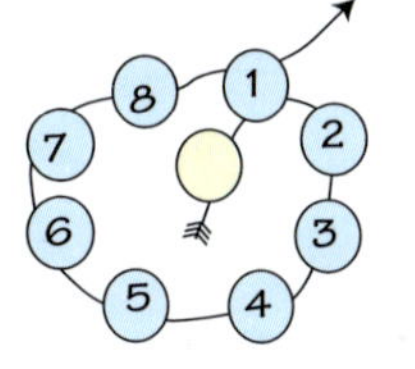

Basic Square Stitch Instructions

Base Rows

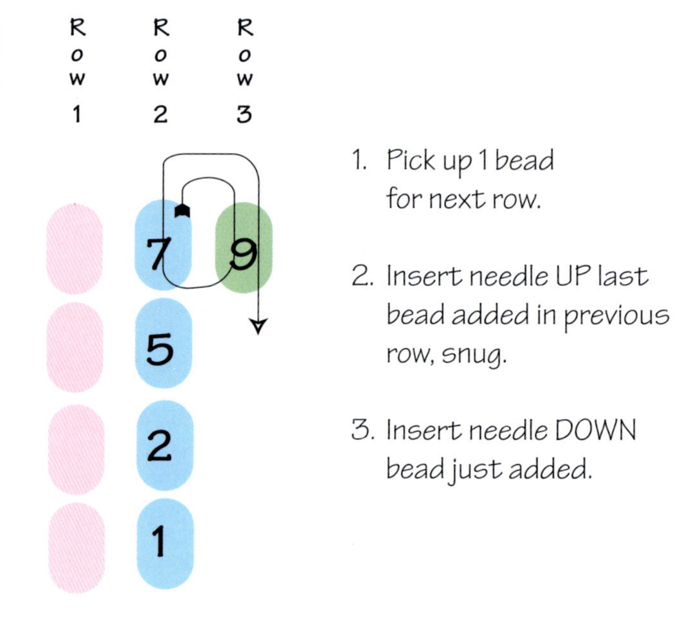

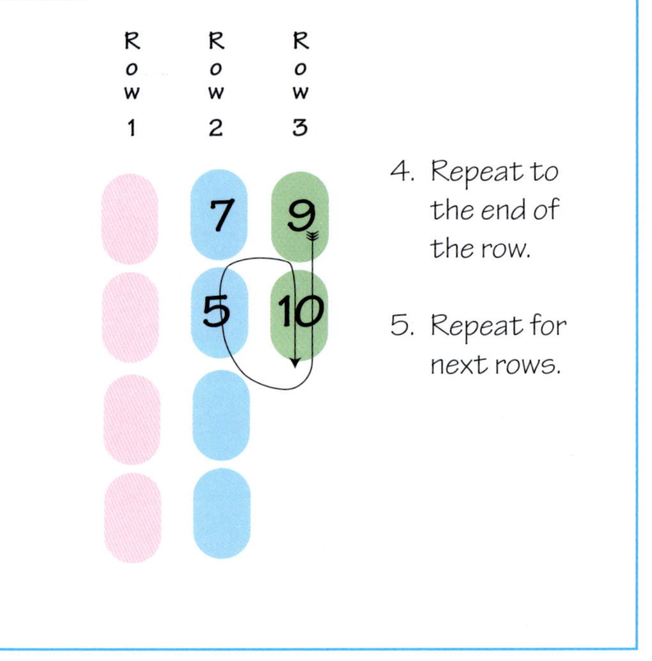

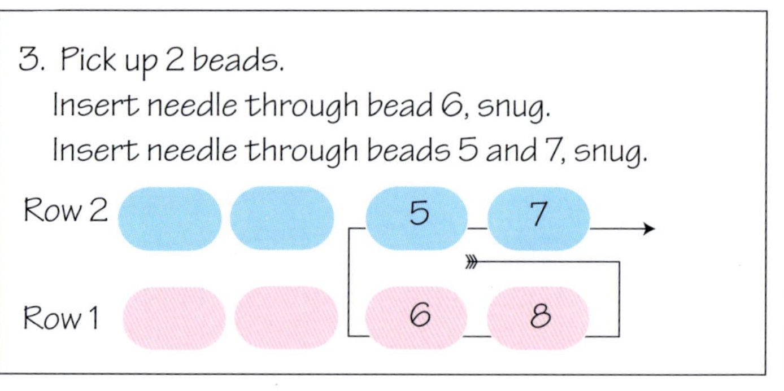

4. Repeat to the end of the base rows.

5. After adding the last 2 beads for your base row, circle stitch the last 2 beads added.

Next Rows

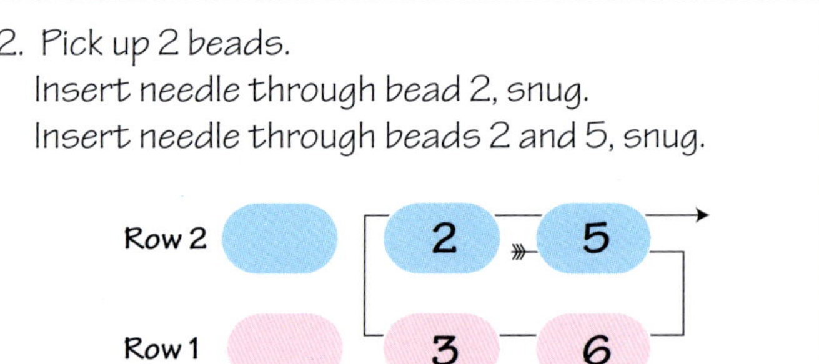

1. Pick up 1 bead for next row.

2. Insert needle UP last bead added in previous row, snug.

3. Insert needle DOWN bead just added.

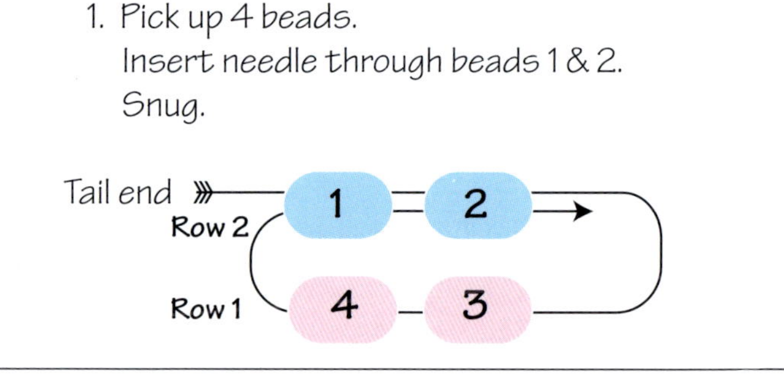

4. Repeat to the end of the row.

5. Repeat for next rows.

Basic Square Stitch Instructions
Continued

Decrease - beginning of row:
Weave thread through previous row to come out of the desire bead. You will want to come out of the bead you want the next bead added to sit next to.

Decreasing - end of Row:
Just stop and start the next row.

Increasing:
To get the best looking finished item. I suggest using the base row method to increase at the beginning or end of a row. This means you must increase 1 bead on 2 rows at the same time. Sometimes you must wait until row 5 is almost done to increase row 4. This eliminates excess edge threads.

Example: Increase beginning of the row.

Create base rows as shown on page 59. This forms rows 1 & 2. You will not add the increase beads on the right until row 3 is started.

Start row 3: Pick up bead 9. Insert needle through bead 7 (to the right) as usual. You can increase on rows 2 & 3 NOW.

Increase beginning of the row: Pick up beads 10 & 11. Insert needle (point left) through bead 9. Insert needle (point right) through beads 7 & 10. Pick up beads 12 & 13. Insert needle through bead 11 (point left). Insert needle through beads 10 & 12 (point right). After the end 2 beads of any rows are added you will need to square up those two beads. Insert needle through bead 13 (point left). Insert needle through bead 12 (point right).

Get into position for the rest of this row: Insert needle through (point left) bead 13 & 11.

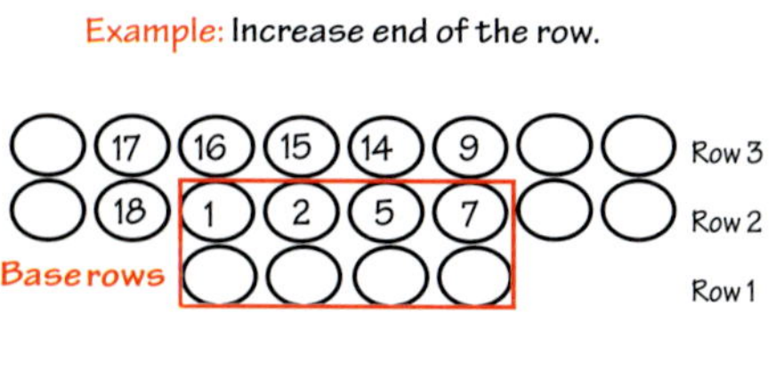

Example: Increase end of the row.

You can only increase when increasing 2 rows at the same time in this method.

You will not add the increase beads on the left of row 2 until you are near the end of row 3 (after bead 16 is added).

Increasing on Rows 2 & 3: Pick up beads 17 & 18. Insert needle through bead 1 (to the right). Insert needle (point left) through beads 16 & 17. Pick up beads 19 & 20. Insert needle through bead 18 (point right). Insert needle through beads 17 & 19 (point left). After the end 2 beads of any rows are added you will need to square up those two beads. Insert needle through bead 20 (point right). Insert needle through bead 19 (point left).

Get into position for the next row and continue on.

MY FAMILY, MY LOVE:

For all their support, patience & unconditional LOVE, I would like to add this very special thank you to my family. I love them all very much, words just could not describe what they all mean to me.

Lee and Mary Jo Schultz (Parents)
David Sova (Husband)
Shane Sova (Son)
Jeannie Sova-Golden (Daughter)
Andrew Golden (Son-in-Law)
Drew Golden (Grandson)

MY STUDENTS, MY FRIENDS:

I was a bit preoccupied (like you didn't know!).
I am very grateful for your encouragements.